Black Relationships Mating & Marriage

Ernestine Walker

Published by:
Essential Information Publications
50 Lexington Avenue-Suite#108
New York, New York 10010

ISBN 0-9631676-1-8
LIBRARY OF CONGRESS CATALOG CARD NUMBER 91-77805

Second Edition

First Essential Information Printing - May, 1992

DEDICATION

This book is dedicated to:

HUSBAND, Willie with love. Closest friend and delightful companion.

SIBLINGS, Bernice, Howard Jr. and Marion & their families so dear, (including Clara and Reese) to whom I am eternally bound by blood, shared experiences and a special kind of feeling.

FAMILY, Contributors of meaning and value to the history of my being. Shinning examples of hope for future generations.

INLAWS, Enduring, substantial and standard bearers of the ethic of keeping the family spirit alive.

FRIENDS, The very special people who share our lives and lovingly reflect our many different aspects.

SPECIAL CONGRATULATIONS TO TERRENCE WHO HOPEFULLY WILL SUPERSEDE THE FINEST VERSION OF HIMSELF.

4

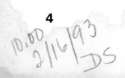

WHAT TOP LEVEL PEOPLE ARE SAYING ABOUT "BLACK RELATIONSHIPS MATING & MARRIAGE."

"An outstanding, valuable, and definitive book about African-American relationships, mating, and marriage. The focus of this book is significant to women and men who are interested in finding compatible relationships."

> Mary Louise Daniel
> Riverdale, New York
> Hospital Executive

"Ms. Walker's book is full of charm and good ideas. I found her writing to be fresh and clear. She addresses the very real problem of man-woman relationships with great skill and warmth."

> Sylvia Evans (Social Worker)
> Queens, New York

"Your system is exactly as you say it, is only better. I wasn't quite sure at first because I never thought that you could control whether or not you found a mate. I was looking for a special kind of woman and wondering if I would ever find her. After using your system for four months, I met her. We plan to marry within the year. It is a fine experience to be engaged to the person that you've been looking for all of your life."

> Ted Fleming (Engineer)
> New Jersey

"The range of emotions it evoked was tremendous. It's a scholarly piece of work. It provides must reading for those of us black or white who desire to keep our relationship portfolio current. It illustrates methods for exploiting established routines; how to establish pathways for doing things that are peripheral to established routines. And how to develop the vision to see and the skill to appreciate the man already in your life and available."

> Claire Hall (Social Worker)
> Bronx, New York

WHAT TOP LEVEL PEOPLE ARE SAYING ABOUT "BLACK RELATIONSHIPS MATING & MARRIAGE."

"I've been looking for a book that would lead me to meeting the man of my dreams. This book is exactly what I wanted."

Leola Harris
Newark, New Jersey

"I don't know exactly how to say this but I just had to share my joy with you. I will admit it, I didn't have very much faith in the whole idea, but last year I decided to use your method. Immediately afterwards I began meeting more eligible men than I had ever met before. As soon as I started meeting the men I knew that things were going to be different. I just didn't usually meet men of this sort. Finally it all narrowed down to Don because for some reason we just seemed to click. We then discovered that we were very similar in so many ways. We started spending all the time together that we could. Don did not live near me at the time. But finally he decided that it would be more convenient to just move so that we could be near each other. We were married last May 20th and everything is just wonderful. I just don't believe it all is really happening. Thank you again for everything."

Corrinne Harrington
Washington, D.C.

"Ms. Walker crafts her book with imagination. Her skills as a writer and social innovator burst forth with wit and forthrightness. I feel she addresses the problem with a new paradigm."

Darlene Linen (Teacher)
New York, NY

FOREWARD

Ernestine Walker has hit a home run because she has touched all bases in the field of relationships. She has touched the tender areas and the critical ones that are needed to make decisions. This book makes the statement "love is a choice we make" so true.

It is the most comprehensive book on this subject I have read. I would recommend it based on the practicums alone because they reach people where they are and move them to where they should be in their personal lives.

The way the book is organized allows the person to move away from the romantic myths into the reality of what is needed to get to the real things that you want in your life with a mate.

It helps you make the hard decisions that move us to our objectives. Ernestine Walker has taken a big subject and problem and done some great research and given it some indepth thought provoking attention that will give others some solutions.

She has given us a fantastic tool to use in personal relationships. It is an important, stimulating book in the area of seeking a mate, taking control of your personal destiny and maintaining a relationship.

This book makes each individual take some responsibilities for the future that they have participated in making and will live with, either alone or with another person.

Elizabeth Sumner-Jiggets
Author/Publisher "Soft Soul"

ACKNOWLEDGEMENTS

We would like to give special thanks to the following people for their support and assistance in producing this book:

Editor

Denise Obie

Cover Design

Sandy Edry

Typesetting

Sandy Edry
CompuEase, Inc.

Indexing

Elton Johnson

THANK YOU TO BLACK WOMEN IN PUBLISHING FOR SUPPORT AND INFORMATION.

ABOUT THE AUTHOR

As early as 1969, Ernestine Walker, who received her B.A. in Psychology from City College, knew that she wanted to know as much as possible about male-female relationships. This realization caused her to constantly read about and study these relationships.

Her diverse professional career consisting of academic, government, and business posts have all been instrumental in fine tuning her awareness about how relationships work. In 1989, when information about the riff between the Black man and women began to surface she found that because of the expertise she had spent twenty years accumulating, she was able to assist with the problem.

That same year she founded National Pairing Systems, creators of a series of phenomenally successful seminars that have helped thousands of Black Men and Women find "exactly right" mates and build satisfying relationships. National Pairing Systems made use of all the information about relationships that she had learned from the research component of her previous company, Scientific Pairing Services. She was therefore able to offer the best methods for finding suitable mates and building satisfying relationships available today. As a trainer for Columbia University, she continued to grow. Her career with New York City Government was highlighted by in 1989 appointment as Women's advisor. She received a Special Recognition Award for serving in that capacity. Although she sees herself primarily as a problem solver, her writing career includes authoring "Why Some People Meet Mates and Friends and others Do Not; writing for both the New York Recorder and the Pittsburgh Courier; and originating a play about the relationships and lives of Black Men and Women. The play received the Audelco Certificate of

Excellence."

Emestine Walker describes herself as an ordinary person who has extraordinary aspirations for both herself and others. She fervently believes that everyone should at least have a loving mate whom they love. Towards this end, she does not dwell on the problems which presently undermine Black male-female relationships. She goes to the heart of the solutions. Commitment to his concept has been her driving force.

Her work has been featured on NBC News, in the Amsterdam News, the Village Voice, and various other newspapers.

In addition to sharing information about male-female relationships, Ernestine Walker enjoys, art, theatre, travelling and music.

She lives in New York City with Willie, her husband of eleven years.

TABLE OF CONTENTS

PART FOUR - SPECIFIC TECHNIQUES FOR MAKING YOUR RELATIONSHIP STICK ONCE YOU FIND A POTENTIAL MATE AND DEALING WITH REJECTION.

PART FIVE - REVEALING DETAILS ABOUT SELECTING THE RIGHT MATE AND IMPROVING YOUR RELATIONSHIP WITH YOUR PRESENT MATE.

Introduction

Its only natural to want another person with whom to share a satisfying relationship. Yet for many African-Americans this simple basic need is extremely difficult and in some instances impossible to fulfill.

Take yourself for example you're an individual with unique qualities and characteristics that almost anyone would treasure. Yet you are having serious problems finding and having positive relationships with members of the opposite sex. And you are not alone. Did you ever ask yourself why is this all happening? And Why now?

After more than twenty years of research, (and I make this statement fully realizing that our Community is not a monolith) it is my conviction that racism is the primary cause of our relationship problems. The secondary causes of our relationship difficulties are the more or less universal problems of inefficient methods of seeking each other out, unrealized expectations, unmet needs, communication breakdown, lack of knowledge about who we are and what we want, lack of information about marriage and relationships - in addition to general incompatibility.

The primary and secondary problems merge and intensify each other.

The end result is what we have, a situation complicated beyond belief. Problems compounded by problems-all exaggerated by very bad press.

I have written this book to help you address these difficulties. It is based on a series of phenomenally successful seminars.

I will share with you techniques designed to help prevent you from wasting away your valuable time trying to find people with whom you are really compatible. Realistic stragies for getting to the definite possibilities and building satisfying relationships with them. No more guess work!

You will notice that the book is structured in a practical hands-on manner. It has been written this way for one reason and one reason only. This approach works!

I set out to solve a painful problem that has lingered for too long in our Community. It is my honest and strong belief that I have done it. No more guesswork!

In addition to a system that delivers results, I offer to you my very best wishes and the means to build in support as you go.

Also, always remember that you are not alone. I am with you all the way.

PART ONE

BASIC POINTS OF REFERENCE FOR MAKING YOUR MOST IMPORTANT DECISIONS ABOUT MATING AND MARRIAGE

Chapter One

DEALING WITH RACISM'S EFFECT ON YOUR OPPORTUNITIES FOR MARRIAGE

BACKGROUND

This chapter will assist you in understanding and dealing with the factors which determine whether or not you will marry. In addition, it will assist you in fully differentiating between those factors which are under your control and those which are not. Finally, it will assist you in terms of taking appropriate action with respect to those factors which you can control.

Your challenge is to view yourself objectively in terms of the characteristics and factors which will determine whether or not you marry. In addition, your challenge is to change or modify those characteristics and factors over which you have some control. Finally, your ultimate challenge is to accept those characteristics and factors over which you have no control.

This chapter requires total honesty in terms of viewing yourself. It also requires the ability to discriminate and make honest assessments.

To utilize this chapter best, analyze your past in relationship to the present. Action is combined with thought in this chapter. Once you arrive at your conclusions, you are to incorporate them into an action plan.

Factors That Determine Whether Or Not You Will Marry And What You Can Do About Those Factors

Whether or not you marry is by no means coincidental. Often it is not entirely determined by your own preferences. For example, the economic and social plight of Black America has a direct and negative impact on your opportunities for marriage.

However, despite the dire conditions, there are many aspects of the mating process that can be successfully managed. We will now focus on the factors outside of race which determine whether or not you will marry — since there is little that you, as an individual, can do about the results of racism.

Many of the factors that will be examined are within your conscious control while others are not. You are empowered to decide whether or not you will marry to the extent that you are aware of and understand all of these factors.

What Are The Factors, Outside of Race, Which Determine Whether Or Not You Will Marry

1. Availability of potential mates.
2. Your level of psychological readiness.
3. Personality factors.
4. Your personal appearance.
5. How selective you are.
6. Concrete data.
7. Miscellaneous factors.

I will now examine these factors in greater detail.

Availability Of Potential Mates

We know for a fact that race, to a large extent, determines how many potential mates are available. Despite this fact, what can you do to increase your opportunities?

Increasing Opportunities

A. You can go to places where there are many more possibilities.

Refer to *"A Going To The Right Places"* (Chapter 8).

B. You can try classified advertising and increase the number of people you will meet.. Refer to the segment on *"Classified Advertising For African-Americans"* (Chapter 6).

C. You can also explore introduction services thereby meeting more people. Refer to the segment on *"A Look At Introduction Services and What They Can Do For You"* (Chapter 7).

D. You can actively decide to be more effective in terms of utilizing the people that you already know to assist you in meeting potential mates. Refer to the section *"How To Use Everything Available To You"* (Chapter 5).

E. Finally, you can become more effective in your ability to relate to the people in your life presently. See *"Selecting the Right Mate And Improving Your Relationship With Your Present Mate"* (Chapter 10)

In summary, any action that you take to increase your pool of prospects increases your possibilities for marriage. For some people, interracial involvement is an option; for others it is not. It is very important that you are clear about where you stand in relationship to this option.

Psychological Readiness

Psychological readiness, which could be an endlessly complicated concept, can for our purposes be defined simply as the readiness to marry.

If you are not ready to marry, it is more than likely you will not. Also, many people who think they want to marry for subtle and complicated reasons really do not.

I cannot overemphasize the importance of psychological readiness in determining whether or not you will marry. Whether or not one is psychologically ready is often due to influences not under his or her immediate control.

Personality Factors

Before I examine personality factors in relationship to how they determine whether or not one will marry, I will define what I mean by personality.

A Definition Of Personality

Everyone has their own definition of personality. In the psychological literature there must be at least 50 different approaches to defining personality. For our purposes, I will simply define personality as consisting of your usual behavior, image, concrete self and the effect that you have on others.

This is most evident in your verbal and non-verbal behavior — your style of communicating with others. Your personality plays an important role in helping to determine whether your relationships will be permanent or temporary. It also helps to determine the quality of your relationships. See Chapter 5 (*"How To Use Everything Available to You"*).

What Can You Do About Your Personality

While you can alter your outer personality through instruction in communication skills, voice, and self-presentation the most lasting and in-depth method of altering your personality is through psychotherapy.

Personal Appearance

Your personal appearance also plays an important role in determining whether or not you will marry. The factors that contribute to your personal appearance are:

1. Your clothing
2. Your hairstyle
   (In many instances your clothing and hairstyle will reflect your degree of Afrocentricity)
3. Your skin
4. Your build
5. Your facial features
6. Your demeanor
7. Your accessories

While there is some basic agreement in terms of what is attractive and what is not attractive in our society, beauty standards may vary from person to person. Also, people vary in the emphasis they place on attractiveness. Although there are some situations which might seem to contradict this premise, it is fairly safe to assume that physical attractiveness is an asset in winning a mate.

What Can You Do About This Factor
Analyze yourself in terms of assets and liabilities. Develop a plan to work on diminishing your liabilities and strengthening your assets. This can be done through altering your hairstyle, cosmetics, build, and demeanor.

How Selective You Are

Your opportunities for marriage exist in direct proportion to how selective you are. Each additional characteristic you require such as wealth, beauty, or superior intelligence automatically eliminates a significant portion of the population. This naturally decreases the number of possibilities available to you. The more people that you feel inclined to reject for whatever reason, the less likely you will be to find someone to marry.

What Can You Do About This Factor
For assistance in managing your tendency to reject others, review "*A New Way of Looking at Others*" (Chapter 4).

I am not advocating that you settle; simply that you realize how severely handicapping it is to be overly selective.

Steps You Can Take To Avoid Being Overly Selective
1. You must really know yourself and now the difference between what you simply want and what you absolutely require.
2. Also, it might help to realize that perfection does not really exist. If you really want to find someone you must prepare yourself to modify your tendency to reject other people.

Concrete Data

Your age, sex, height and weight play parts in determining your marriage opportunities. Why? Most people begin their search for a mate with definite preferences in these areas. Therefore, concrete data is important as a sorting out process.

Although all of the factors are important concrete data deserves serious consideration, since often it can determine whether or not the supply and demand aspects of the mating process work in your favor.

What Can You Do About These Factors

With the exception of weight, there isn't very much one can do about concrete data.

Miscellaneous Factors

For a cluster of reasons, statistically speaking, people who have married previously are more likely to marry than individuals who have never married.

In addition, factors such as status, wealth, status professions and celebrity status also increase your possibilities for marriage.

PRACTICUM

SELF QUIZ

1. What are the factors that determine whether or not you will marry?

2. What are the factors that determine whether or not you are physically attractive?

3. How does your selectivity influence the numbers of potential mates available to you?

4. How can you increase the number of potential mates available to you?

5. Why are general statistics relatively unimportant in determining whether or not you will find a suitable mate?

FUNCTIONAL EXERCISES

1. In terms of the factors, outside of race, that determine whether or not you will marry, list your strengths.
   A. _____
   B. _____
   C. _____
   D. _____
   E. _____

2. List the areas where you need work.
   A. _____
   B. _____

C. _____
D. _____
E. _____

3. List the actions that you plan to take regarding the factors over which you have control.
   A. _____
   B. _____
   C. _____
   D. _____
   E. _____

4. List the obstacles that may prevent you from reaching your goals.
   A. _____
   B. _____
   C. _____
   D. _____
   E. _____

5. List the steps that you are taking to deal with these obstacles.
   A. _____
   B. _____
   C. _____
   D. _____
   E. _____

KEY QUESTIONS

1. Is it necessary to alter my personal appearance?

2. What actions do I plan to take?

3. Do I need psychotherapy to increase my level of psychological readiness?

4. Am I overly selective?

5. Where do I stand in terms of interracial involvement?

CHAPTER HIGHLIGHTS

1. Race is an important determiner of opportunities or lack of opportunities for marriage.

2. Despite racism many aspects of the mating process can be successfully managed.

3. The more you know about the factors determining whether or not you will marry, the greater your opportunity for exerting conscious control over those factors.

4. Even though you need not settle for less than you desire, you can greatly increase your possibilities for marriage by not being overly selective.

Chapter Two

SELF KNOWLEDGE AS A POWERFUL TOOL

BACKGROUND

In addition to the sad results of racism, many people fail in their relationships and marriages because they do not have a clear understanding of who they are, who they are not, what they want and what they do not want. This chapter will assist you in clarifying these very important questions.

Your challenge is to be totally candid in terms of looking at who you are instead of who you would like to be. In addition, your challenge is to honestly admit to yourself what you really want instead of what you feel you should, or would like, to want. In short, avoid self-deception.

This is not an action chapter. You succeed with this chapter to the extent that you are willing to be totally honest with yourself and reasonable in terms of what you require. A great deal of thought and concentration are needed.

Knowing Yourself And What You Want

Who are you? What kind of person do you want? You need to know the answers to these questions because self-knowledge gives you power. You know what is for you and what is not. You therefore know who to seek out and who to avoid. Many mating mistakes are made because people do not know themselves. These mistakes are often costly, both on a material and emotional level.

Let's now look at who you are and what you want in terms of concrete data, degree of Afrocentricity, personal appearance, socio-economic status, personal characteristics, interests and general belief system.

Concrete Data

Concrete data simply consists of your age, race, height and build and the age, race, height and build of the person you wish to meet. Your requirements in age may range from slightly younger than your own age to older. You may have specific requirements in terms of build and height.

Regarding race, you may be interested in meeting only other Black-Americans, or you may be open to interracial involvement. You serve yourself to the extent that you are aware of the pros and cons of either option, which will vary from person to person.

Afrocentricity

Not only must you know who you are, you must know where you stand in regards to your Blackness since there are vast differences in the ways in which Black-Americans view their Blackness and its many implications.

If a relationship is to succeed, there must also be compatibility in terms of the degree of Afrocentricity. If large differences exist there will be trouble. This is especially true if children are planned.

Personal Appearance

Your own personal appearance and the personal appearance of the person you would like to meet may range from very attractive, to

Self Knowledge As A Powerful Tool

attractive, fairly attractive, average, not particularly attractive, or unattractive. In terms of what you want you may want to meet someone more or less physically attractive than you are or you may wish to meet someone on your own level. You might even desire someone whose personal appearance reflects Afrocentricity. Generally, in most areas, unless there is some trade off possibility, what you can demand to a large extent depends on what you have to offer. It is extremely important that you are honest with yourself about your own personal appearance and the importance of personal appearance to you.

Socio-Economic Status

Socio-economic status is significant since it often determines an individual's outlook on other significant areas of life. Socio-economic status may be indicated by level of income, occupation, background and levels of education.

For convenience, people can be divided into upper, middle and lower classes. However, there are many gradations and variations within these groups. Generally, in terms of finding a compatible mate, similarity in socio-economic status will usually result in greater compatibility. This, however, is not always true.

Personal Characteristics

There are many different kinds of personal characteristics. Personal characteristics may include intelligence, optimism , self-confidence, permissiveness, sincerity, assertiveness or the opposite of these traits.

You are usually aware of your personal characteristics through accumulated self-knowledge and from what other people say or have said about you.

The personal characteristics that you are seeking in a mate, may or may not be those that you possess yourself yet they are an important indicator of your needs. It is very important to be fully aware of the traits or characteristics that you need to find in the person you will marry.

Interests

Usually as an adult individual you have developed one or more activities or past times in which you have an interest. Your interests may range from sports, the arts, science, collecting items, reading, history, gardening, television to everything or nothing in particular.

In terms of what you want, how important is it that you and your mate have interests in common. Ideally, it is highly desirable. In fact, some people require that their mates share their interests. However, in reality it is not an absolute necessity. A couple may have different interests and still maintain a successful marriage if they are compatible in other important areas.

Your General Belief System

What do you feel is important? Important life goals might be getting money, spiritual growth, personal advancement, acquiring power, maintaining a successful family life, happiness, civil rights, social change, gaining knowledge or something other than what is stated here.

Ideally, there should be some agreement between marriage partners in terms of the overall purpose in life. Some people require it. While you need not be in complete harmony with your mate on every detail, it is most important that there are no sharp conflicts.

Mutuality In Terms Of Attitude Towards Marriage

Although the person you meet may be exactly what you want in every other way, his or her attitude towards marriage itself must not clash with yours or there will be difficulty. Attitudes towards marriage may range from very interested to somewhat interested, undecided, uninterested, or positively against it.

If you really want to marry your intended spouse should eventually feel the same way about marriage that you do. Not only must he or she want to marry, but he or she must want to marry you. If not, you must move on. One year is sufficient time for a person to decide whether or not he or she wants to marry you.

We will now look at:

What You Don't Want

During the course of a lifetime you probably have discovered one or more characteristics that you dislike. Often these dislikes are based on childhood and/or later experiences. Your dislikes are also an important indicator of your needs — what you need to avoid. In a relationship it is very important not to push these buttons. Also connected with characteristics that you dislike are habits that you will not tolerate. For some it might be drugs, for others it may be alcohol. The possibilities are many.

In addition to knowing what you want it is extremely important to be absolutely clear on what you don't want. You are urged to take a hard look at what you want to avoid in life and in relationships. These aversions should be considered at least as carefully as your desires.

PRACTICUM

SELF QUIZ

1. Outside of race what are the key indicators of who you are?

2. What is meant by concrete data?

3. What are the three categories that your requirements for an ideal mate may include?

4. In addition to what you want and who you are, what else is important?

FUNCTIONAL EXERCISES

1. Make a list of those requirements upon which you will compromise.
   A. _____
   B. _____
   C. _____
   D. _____
   E. _____

2. Make a list of those upon which you will not compromise.
   A. _____
   B. _____
   C. _____
   D. _____
   E. _____

3. Rank your requirements in the order of their priority.
   A. _____

B. _____
C. _____
D. _____
E. _____

4. List the characteristics which you have that others might find desirable.
   A. _____
   B. _____
   C. _____
   D. _____
   E. _____

KEY QUESTIONS

1. What kinds of people have I had unsuccessful relationships with?

2. What kinds of people do I dislike?

3. What am I trying to avoid in life?

4. What am I trying to avoid in relationships?

5. What characteristics would be difficult for me to tolerate?

6. What habits would be difficult for me to tolerate?

CHAPTER HIGHLIGHTS

1. Finding a suitable mate will be very difficult if you do not have a very clear idea of who you are.

2. There are several key indicators of who you are.

3. It is also important to know what you don't want.

4. It is very important to avoid being a perfectionist.

Chapter Three

WHAT YOU NEED TO KNOW ABOUT LOVE AND MARRIAGE

BACKGROUND

If you plan to marry you need a realistic perception of love and marriage and how they relate to you. In addition, you need to analyze the pros and cons of both so that you have a realistic understanding of what they are and what they are not.

Marriage means different things to different people. It can either be a negative or a positive experience. It can either be comfortable or tense and disturbing. It can either add to your psychological well-being or detract from it. In addition, if you plan to marry, it is most important to decide upon the kind of marriage that you want to have since not all marriages are alike.

This chapter will assist you in developing a realistic attitude about what marriage is and what it is not. In addition, it takes a hard look at some of the advantages and disadvantages of love and marriage. It will also assist you in clarifying some of your internal blocks so that you will focus on eliminating them.

Your challenge is to absorb all the information possible. In addition, your challenge is to modify your attitudes in order to align them with the realities of marriage, if you plan to marry. At the same time, you are to remain essentially who you are.

This is not an action chapter. Rather than act, it is most

important that you fully absorb all of the material.

Read and review this information frequently.

First let us examine some of the basic reasons people marry.

Some Important Reasons Why People Marry

1. They might fall in love and marry.
2. They might marry to have a home and family.
3. They might marry to increase their wealth or status.
4. They might marry because it is expected of them.
5. They might marry because of peer or parental pressure.
6. They might marry because they are lonely.
7. They might marry also for a combination of the above reasons.
   The reasons for marriage may vary from person to person.

Some Important Reasons Why People Might Not Marry

1. They remain in relationships that do not lead to marriage for too long a period of time. If a person really wants too marry, the longer he or she remains in a relationship that will not lead to marriage, the more he or she is eliminating the opportunity for marriage. This is true for both Black men and women.
2. Both Black men and women may not marry for financial reasons.
3. They may have other obligations.
   However, the most important reasons why people do not marry are:
1. Lack of opportunities and
2. Lack of psychological readiness.
   Let's now examine both:

Lack Of Opportunities

It is difficult if not impossible to marry if you do not have sufficient opportunities to select a suitable mate.

Some of the reasons why people might lack opportunities are:
1. They are overly selective and eliminate their opportunities.
2. They are not in the position to meet eligible persons.
3. Statistically the odds are stacked against them. Black women in particular, may lack opportunities because of the decreasing number of eligible Black men.

Psychological Readiness

Psychological readiness as we previously discussed plays a large part in determining whether or not you will marry.

Factors that might contribute to lack of psychological readiness are:
1. Emotional difficulties.
2. Previous negative mating experiences.
3. The negative mating experiences of others.

We will now look at marriage in terms of both its negative and positive aspects — we will also examine its limitations.

How Marriages May Vary

Marriages may vary in terms of:
1. The amount of time spent together.
2. How that time is used.
3. The division of tasks.
4. Where financial responsibility lies.
5. Whether or not polygamy is acceptable.
6. Whether or not there are offspring.
7. The role of sex.
8. The amount of personal freedom granted each individual.
9. How the home is used.

What Are The Positive Aspects Of Marriage

1. There is the possibility it may improve your financial status. Women more often than men have the opportunity to upgrade themselves financially through marriage.
2. It may offer you an opportunity for safer sex. This is only true if there is fidelity in the marriage.
3. Usually companionship is a by-product of marriage.
4. In marriage you have the legal rights of a spouse.

What Are Some Of The Negative Aspects Of Marriage

1. Marriage may become a negative experience and create the need for a divorce.
2. Marriage may worsen your financial situation since sometimes divorce results in alimony payments.
3. If children result from the marriage, they may not live up to your expectations.
4. Marriage may worsen latent psychological problems.
5. In marriage you have the legal responsibilities and restraints of a spouse.

What Are The Limitations Of Marriage

1. Marriage often cannot solve deep seated emotional difficulties.
2. Marriage may not offer you constant sexual satisfaction.
3. It may not offer you constant excitement.
4. Marriage alone cannot make you happy. *Only you can make you happy.*
5. Marriage may not offer you lasting love.

We will now examine love.

ON LOVE

People May Fall In Love For The Following Reasons

1. A pleasing appearance.
2. An intriguing personality.
3. Proximity.
4. Because of an individual's status.
5. Because of an individual's communication skills.

Actually, the reasons that people fall in love are intricate and complex and closely tied to their psychological readiness and individual conditioning.

Why Is Love Important

1. Many people require love before marriage.
2. If you are loved, it places you at an advantage in a relationship.
3. Love creates positive feelings.

Why Love May Be Unimportant

1. It may be based on superficial reasons.
2. For centuries throughout the world many people have participated in arranged marriages despite the absence of love.
3. Love is not usually based on reason and objective factors.
4. Love may not last.

What Are Some Of The Disadvantages Of Requiring Love As A Pre-Requisite To Marriage

1. It may impede you in your search for a mate, since it may not be possible to find someone you love who is also compatible with you.
2. It may cause you to marry someone totally unsuitable.

Limitations Of Love

1. Love cannot create compatibility where there is none.
2. Love cannot solve deep seated emotional difficulties.
3. Often love cannot survive a long rigorous exposure to reality. This is possibly the reason that love sometimes does not survive marriage.
4. Our ability to love one another is adversely affected by racism.

How Does Love Relate To You In Your Search For A Mate

This is an individual decision. You are the one who needs to decide whether or not love is important to you and if it is, how important it is.

PRACTICUM

SELF QUIZ

1. Why is psychological readiness important?

2. What is a major reason both Black men and Black women may not marry?

3. Why do most people marry?

4. What are the most important reasons which cause people not to marry?

5. How significant is love in terms of motivation to marry?

FUNCTIONAL EXERCISES

1. Decide whether you want to marry. If you want to marry, list the reasons why you want to marry.
   A. _____
   B. _____
   C. _____
   D. _____
   E. _____

2. List all the reservations you may have about marrying.
   A. _____
   B. _____
   C. _____
   D. _____
   E. _____

3. List all the marriages that you consider to be successful.

    A. _____

    B. _____

    C. _____

    D. _____

    E. _____

4. List all of the reasons why you think they are successful.

    A. _____

    B. _____

    C. _____

    D. _____

    E. _____

5. If previously married, list the most obvious reasons why the marriage ended.

    A. _____

    B. _____

    C. _____

    D. _____

    E. _____

6. What was your role in the process?

    A. _____

    B. _____

    C. _____

    D. _____

    E. _____

7. List some of the actions you are taking to prevent a recurrence of these difficulties.

    A. _____

    B. _____

    C. _____

    D. _____

E. _____

F. _____

KEY QUESTIONS

1. What personal characteristics do you have that will contribute to the success of a marriage?

2. In which areas do your liabilities lie?

3. What kind of marriage do you want to have?

4. How do you intend to bring it about?

5. How do you see your role in the marriage?

6. How do you see your spouse's role?

7. Do you think that your expectations are realistic?

8. Do you have any difficulties with any of the following?
   A.   Sharing your life on a daily basis.
   B.   Offering emotional support.
   C.   Experiencing intimacy.

9. How do you feel about love in relationship to marriage?

10. How can you dilute the effects of racism on your marriage or love relationship?

CHAPTER HIGHLIGHTS

1. For some people, love and marriage are synonymous.

2. There are numerous pitfalls involved in terms of marrying for love without considering compatibility.

3. You need to make a decision about how important love is to you.

4. There are limitations in terms of what both love and marriage can do.

5. Black women may lack opportunities for marriage because of the decreasing number of eligible Black men.

Chapter Four

DEVELOPING THE RIGHT MIND SET - DESPITE RACISM

BACKGROUND

Because of the effects of racism, you may have a tendency to devalue yourself and others like yourself. This chapter will offer methods and techniques to assist in modifying the tendency to devalue both yourself and others. In addition, this chapter will assist you in gaining pleasure from the process of seeking a mate, which can either be a joyous adventure or drudgery. One can succeed at this process or fail dismally.

This chapter is challenging in that it requires you to modify some of your basic attitudes about yourself and others. It is difficult, but it can be done. The facts that you provide yourself with will help to build the attitudes that are most effective. While I certainly do not advocate pairing with a mate that you really do not want, your challenge is to avoid being overly rejecting.

Take your time to reflect and give the functional exercises and key questions a great deal of thought.

Feel free to rely on photographs and documents to reinforce your positive thoughts about yourself. If necessary, gain the assistance of others to help you remember past successes and victories.

How To Think About Your Search For A Mate

- You are most likely to succeed at this process of finding the right mate if you see it as fun. Once you view it from that vantage point it will be easier to persist and succeed.
- Line up your expectations with reality. Finding a suitable mate is a difficult task and might not be something that you can accomplish immediately. Remember: it is just as important to find the right person as it is to marry.
- Expect to succeed. Often our expectations play an important role in determining whether or not we succeed. Despite the present problems in the Black community you can still find the right mate. See yourself as a professional, systematically involved in a process. This is not a haphazard procedure.
- Become process oriented. That is, become as involved in the process as you are in the end result. This technique will allow you to become more relaxed.
- Develop some pertinent sub-goals. Although the goal is to meet and marry the right person, a suitable sub-goal could be to meet as many eligible people as possible and to enjoy the time you spend with them.
- Even though, in all probability, you will marry, have an interesting plan for your life should you not marry. The alternate plan should be just as attractive as the marriage plan. The reason for this is obvious.

A New Way Of Looking At Yourself

Often we tend to devalue ourselves, our lives and our accomplishments because we have been devalued.

With the exception of young adolescent girls, in a basically Eurocentric country, it may be difficult for some of us to maintain our self-esteem. To counteract the negative influences it often helps to have a sense of our historical significance. Once we have this, we can be absolutely clear about the fact that we have made some important contributions to this country. See the recommended readings and bibliographies for specific resources, which will assist us in seeing ourselves in a more positive light. This is very important knowledge when one is involved in a search for a mate because how we see ourselves influences to a large extent how others perceive us.

Additional Techniques For Helping To Build Self-Esteem

1. Focus on the positive aspects of your life, personality and relationships.
2. Be specific and really get in touch with the good in your life.
3. If you have difficulty recalling the positive, you might begin to keep records of your accomplishments and document them as they occur.
4. You might also wish to accumulate evidence and document past accomplishments.
5. You may wish to involve others by asking them to target your positive characteristics.
6. The functional exercises go into more specific techniques for seeing yourself in a positive light.
7. Although psychotherapy is the most intensive method for raising your level of self-esteem, the exercises prescribed in the functional exercise section are very effective actions that you can take on your own behalf.

A New Way Of Looking At Others

Often, for the very same reasons that you may perceive yourself in a negative way, you may also place a negative value on others.

Obviously, the more people you reject, the more your opportunities will decrease.

Some Hidden Reasons Why We May Reject Others

1. The press has not been kind to us. This may cause us to devalue each other.
2. We fear others may reject us.

3. We may reject others because we may be emotionally unavailable for a close relationship.
4. We may reject others simply because of their availability to us.
5. We may reject others because we are seeking perfection, which is unattainable.

Some More Obvious Reasons Why We May Reject Others

1. We believe that we can or should do better.
2. They are unattractive and we really do not want to be associated with them.
3. They may be attractive but for some reason we feel that we are not compatible with them.

Often we would not reject the very same person
- if we fully understood the effects of racism.
- at some future date.
- in a different situation.
- if we knew more about him or her.
- under a different set of circumstances.
- if he or she made some minor changes.
- if we had more information.

If you really want to develop long term relationships you might consider giving others the benefit of the doubt before rejecting them.

For specific techniques in terms of managing your tendency to reject others see the *Key Questions* segment.

PRACTICUM

SELF QUIZ

1. What is a major reason why we may reject ourselves and others?

2. What is one cause of being overly rejecting?

3. How can you diminish your tendency to be overly rejecting?

4. What are four different methods that you can use to raise your level of self-esteem?

5. How does your tendency to reject others tie in with the tendency to be self-rejecting?

6. What is a benefit of being process oriented in your search for a mate?

FUNCTIONAL EXERCISES

1. List eight qualities that you like about yourself.
   A. _____
   B. _____
   C. _____
   D. _____
   E. _____
   F. _____
   G. _____
   H. _____

2. List six positive qualities that others have praised you for.

A. _____
B. _____
C. _____
D. _____
E. _____
F. _____

3. List four of your natural assets.

A. _____
B. _____
C. _____
D. _____

4. List four assets that you have acquired.

A. _____
B. _____
C. _____
D. _____

5. List four rare skills that you have.

A. _____
B. _____
C. _____
D. _____

6. List four personal victories that you have won in life.

A. _____
B. _____
C. _____
D. _____

7. List four major successes in your life.

A. _____
B. _____

C. _____
D. _____

8. List two minor successes.
   A. _____
   B. _____

9. List four actions that you can take that will make seeking a mate more fun.
   A. _____
   B. _____
   C. _____
   D. _____

10. Think of more positive traits and characteristics.
   A. _____
   B. _____
   C. _____
   D. _____
   E. _____

11. Reward yourself for each one that you think of.

A NEW WAY OF LOOKING AT OTHERS

KEY QUESTIONS

If you ask yourself the following questions, you will decrease the number of people that you feel inclined to reject.

1. Am I rejecting this person because of all the bad press about us?

2. Is there a possibility that I would not reject this person if I knew him or her better?

3. Is there a possibility that I would not reject him or her at some other time?

4. Is there a possibility that I would not reject this person if I knew for sure that the kind of person I am seeking is not available?

5. What positive traits does this person have?

6. How can I enjoy myself with him or her?

7. What do we have in common?

8. What other situation would maximize his or her potential?

9. In which areas might my negative opinions change?

10. Am I rejecting this person simply because he or she is available to me?

11. Would I like him or her if he or she were not available?

12. Am I rejecting this person out of fear that he or she will reject me?

13. What minor changes on his (or her) part would cause me to modify my rejection?

14. Am I willing to take the risk of speaking to this person about those changes?

CHAPTER HIGHLIGHTS

1. The dire effects of racism need not cause you to reject yourself or others.

2. Lack of self-esteem is a severely limiting factor in your search for a mate.

Developing The Right Mind Set - Despite Racism

3. It is possible for you to build your level of self-esteem.

4. If you see seeking a mate as fun, you are more likely to succeed at the process.

PART TWO

POTENT METHODS FOR MOBILIZING YOUR TOTAL STORE OF RESOURCES TO HELP YOU REACH YOUR GOALS.

Chapter Five

HOW TO USE EVERYTHING AVAILABLE TO YOU

BACKGROUND

As an African-American, finding a mate may not be easy. Therefore you will need to use everything available to you. This chapter, which is about resources, will assist you in identifying and coordinating the total sum of the resources which are available to you. This will make the mate selection process easier and more efficient.

In addition, this chapter assists you in assessing whether or not psychotherapy — which is a special kind of people resource — might be of value to you in dealing with some of the result of racism and finding a mate just right for you..

Your challenge is not only to target the assistance that you may need, but to be willing to use it. In addition, your challenge is to use this assistance if needed in the most effective manner possible.

Finally, your challenge is to honestly assess whether or not you can utilize psychotherapy as a resource in your search for a mate.

Although this chapter calls for some thought and analysis, it is primarily an action chapter. Numerous optional self-management forms have been included in this work. They are designed to move you into action. In all probability, you will be able to take the required actions. However, if you have any difficulty, you can make use of these forms since they have a proven history of success.

RESOURCES

People Resources

Resources may be internal or external, they may be tangible or intangible. One of your most important resources are people resources — especially the people you already know. Almost every person that you know knows someone suitable for you. Not only does each known person know someone eligible, often he or she knows someone with enough basic similarities to you to make a good relationship possible.

Who Are The People In Your Address Book

People in your address book fall into three major categories — relatives, friends and associates.

Relatives

Usually your relatives will be most motivated to assist you in finding a mate. In fact, many of them may already be involved in the process.

Friends

Sometimes friends will be motivated to assist you. However, some will be more motivated than others.

Associates

While your associates may have less of a vested interest in helping you find a suitable mate, it is most important not to overlook them. In many instances they may need to be asked to assist you.

How Can These People Assist You

1. They can be an invaluable source of support.
2. They can offer you direct assistance in producing prospects.

How Do You Involve Them In the Process

1. Make a direct request for their assistance.
2. Be specific about the kind of mate that you are seeking.
3. Set aside a definite time and place to meet the person or persons that they suggest. (You could possibly invite them to a dinner party.)

What Is Your Most Effective Follow Up Activity

1. Reward yourself for each contact you make. It could be a gift of something you really want. This reward system will reinforce and motivate you.
2. It is very important to reward the people who begin to produce possibilities. They will then be more than willing to continue their assistance. You can use your best judgement about how you will reward them.

An Additional Possibility

Is there the possibility that you already know someone suitable for marriage? Often we feel that we do not know anyone suitable when in reality we do. It often is simply a matter of removing some of our internal barriers so that we can perceive reality more accurately. Review "*New Ways of Looking At Others*" (Chapter 4) in order to ensure that you are not rejecting real possible mates.

PSYCHOTHERAPY

We will now examine psychotherapy. You will need to decide whether or not it will be useful to you in your search for a mate.

Because of the current strife in the Black community, we need to use every resource which is available to stabilize ourselves, our relationships and our families. Sadly enough, because of a cultural aversion, many of us are locked out of using psychotherapy as an advancement tool.

If I do nothing else during the course of this book except to break through your barrier (if you have one) to using psychotherapy (if you need it), it will be well worth the price of this book.

There are numerous kinds of psychotherapy: including behavioral therapy, activity therapy, medication therapy and verbal therapies. For our purposes, when I refer to psychotherapy, I am referring to the verbal therapies.

What Happens During Psychotherapy

Psychotherapy is talking about what is going on in your life and your feelings about these events and persons to a trained therapist.

How Does It Relate To You
In Your Search For A Mate

1. It can assist you in becoming psychologically ready.
2. It can minimize your tendency to reject others.
3. It can assist in raising your level of self-esteem.
4. It can assist you in dealing with rejection.
5. It can assist you in your relationships with the opposite sex.

Who Practices Psychotherapy
And What Are Their Qualifications

A wide range of people from ministers to lawyers to lay people may practice psychotherapy since there are no legal restrictions on the use of the title "Psychotherapist." However, the professionals most qualified and most appropriate are the Psychiatrist, the Psychologist and the Social Worker.

A **Psychiatrist** is a medical doctor who also has 3 years additional training in Psychiatry.

A **Psychologist** has a Ph.D. in Psychology and is state licensed.

A **Social Worker** has a Masters Degree in social work and is state certified.

Some of these professionals, in addition to the above qualifications, are also trained in psychoanalysis.

Fees

The fees vary according to the kind of professional you decide to use, taking into account the education and training. Fees may also vary according to where the therapy takes place, the overhead of the professional that you select and according to your financial means.

How Often Do You Go

The number of visits to your therapist can range from once a month to several times a week.

How Long Does It Last

Therapy can last for several months or for several years; it depends on the kinds of problems and the kind of therapy.

What Psychotherapy Can Do In Addition To Assisting You In Relating To A Mate

It can assist you:
1. with crises in your life.
2. in solving problems that may develop.
3. in coming to terms with deep seated problems.
4. in changing some personality traits.

How Psychotherapy Can Assist You After You Marry

1. It can help you adjust to a mate.
2. It can play a preventive role in terms of minimizing the possibilities of problems developing.

What Psychotherapy Cannot Do

1. It cannot change who you are.

2. It cannot make you happy all the time.
3. It cannot create compatibility where there is none.

How To Determine If You Need Psychotherapy

1. You are often anxious.
2. You are often depressed.
3. You have difficulty holding jobs.
4. You have low self-esteem.
5. You are constantly rejecting others.
6. Others are consistently rejecting you.
7. You have difficulty with relationships.
8. You have sexual difficulties.
9. You have difficulty sleeping.
10. You are functioning at a capacity far less then you are capable.
11. You are often angry for no real reason.
12. You are inappropriately angry for real reasons.
13. You often find yourself in abusive relationships.
14. You remain in an abusive relationship.
15. You are in an extremely stressful situation.

How To Determine If You Need Psychotherapy And The Type Of Psychotherapy Best Suited To You

This might involve consultation, referrals, reading on your part and other methods of exploration. Some excellent resources for identifying and accessing the appropriate treatment are included in this book (See "*Recommended Readings and Selected Bibliography* ").

Finally, not everyone needs psychotherapy, but if you feel you can use it, see it as a sound investment of your time and funds.

PRACTICUM

SELF QUIZ

1. What is one advantage of considering people you already know as sources of meeting potential mates?

2. What roles can the people you already know play in your search for a mate?

3. How can you motivate the people you already know to assist you?

4. Does everyone need psychotherapy?

FUNCTIONAL EXERCISES

1. Make a list of friends, relatives, and associates who might know someone suitable for you to meet.
   A. _____
   B. _____
   C. _____
   D. _____
   E. _____
   F. _____
   G. _____
   H. _____
   I. _____

J. _____

2. List specific means of contacting them.

Person	Contact Method
A. _____	_____
B. _____	_____
C. _____	_____
D. _____	_____
E. _____	_____
F. _____	_____
G. _____	_____
H. _____	_____
I. _____	_____
J. _____	_____

3. Set aside a definite time for contacting them.

Person	Phone Number	Contact Date	Contact Time
A. _____	_____	_____	_____
B. _____	_____	_____	_____
C. _____	_____	_____	_____
D. _____	_____	_____	_____
E. _____	_____	_____	_____
F. _____	_____	_____	_____
G. _____	_____	_____	_____
H. _____	_____	_____	_____
I. _____	_____	_____	_____
J. _____	_____	_____	_____

4. Reward yourself after each contact.

5. List specific methods of rewarding them.

Person	Reward
A. _____	_____
B. _____	_____
C. _____	_____

How To Use Everything Available To You

D. _____ _____

E. _____ _____

F. _____ _____

G. _____ _____

H. _____ _____

I. _____ _____

J. _____

KEY QUESTIONS

1. Who are additional people that I might contact?

2. What are additional resources that I might use?

3. Am I rewarding myself for each additional idea?

4. What are my honest feelings about using psychotherapy as a resource in my search for a mate?

CHAPTER HIGHLIGHTS

1. You need not struggle through the process of finding a mate alone.

2. There are resources in close proximity which you may use to make the process easier and more efficient.

3. It is important that you plan a system of rewards for the people who will assist you.

4. Some individuals can increase the possibility that they will marry by utilizing psychotherapy as a resource.

PART THREE

SPECIFIC WORKABLE METHODS AND SYSTEMS
FOR FINDING AN "EXACTLY RIGHT" MATE.

Chapter Six

WHY THE PERSONAL CLASSIFIED ADS AND HOW TO USE THEM

BACKGROUND

This chapter will provide you with background information about using classified advertising in the personals. In addition, it will assist you in terms of clarifying your desires, personality and personal dislikes in a concise way so that you are proficient at writing personal classified ads. Finally, it will assist you if you decide to record a personal classified ad.

Should you decide to use this method of seeking a mate, your challenge is to learn how to present yourself in an honest, yet realistic way. In addition, your challenge is to describe yourself without bragging or belittling yourself.

Your challenge is also to learn how to describe what you want and don't want without being overly demanding or critical. Finally, your challenge is to take the necessary steps to improve your voice — if there is a need — should you decide to record your ads.

Should you decide to utilize this method of seeking a mate, constant practice will be very important to you. Write and rewrite your ad until you develop an ability for writing short, concise sentences that will attract the kind of person you wish to meet. Since you will need to think about your approach, this is both a thought and action chapter.

Personal Classified Advertising

Lately the personal classified advertising method of seeking a mate has grown in popularity in the Black community. This growth is possibly due to the fact that there are now fewer community and family structures and mechanisms to serve this purpose.

However like any other mode of seeking a mate, this method has its pros and cons.

What Are Some Advantages Of Using Personal Classified Advertising In Your Search For The Right Mate

1. You can meet more people than you would by using the more conventional methods.
2. You can control the expectations of the other person.
3. You can impact with your personality prior to meeting the other person.

What Are Some Of The Disadvantages

1. It takes time and must be done correctly.
2. You will need to experiment with the kind of ad which works best for you.
3. It can be costly.
4. You might meet someone that you do not want to meet. However, this might happen with any method that you choose. You can diminish the possibility of unwanted incidents occurring by exercising the same kind of caution that you would exercise when meeting any stranger under any circumstances.

How Do You Write An Effective Classified Personal Ad

Although there are numerous approaches to writing a classified personal ad, the method which I am outlining has proven to be very effective.

What are the seven components of a person classified ad that works?

1. An attention getting heading.
2. Some indication of who you are.
3. Some indication of what you want.
4. Some indication of what you don't want.
5. A brief allusion to your liabilities if any.
6. Emphasis on your positive qualities.
7. A provocative ending.

Let's examine these parts in greater detail.

An Attention Getting Heading

In order to maximize the ability of your ad to attract attention it is a good idea to have a heading that commands immediate attention by raising a question or making an overt statement. It is usually a good idea to put your heading in bold capital letters.

Who You Are

Your ad should indicate who you are in terms of physical appearance, profession, age, race, temperament and other relevant factors. Be brief and selective in terms of the information that you give. Include only the information that you consider most important in terms of who you are.

What You Want

This section should list your requirements in terms of physical appearance, profession, age, race, temperament and other important items. You may or may not opt to become involved on an interracial level. This part of your ad should reflect this decision. If personality requirements are more important that other other factors this should be indicated. Don't try to list everything. List only your most important requirements.

What You Don't Want

This section of your ad is important. If you have strong dislikes, and many of us do, it is an excellent idea to state this in your ad. This will serve to eliminate people you do not want to meet. In the long run this saves you valuable time. In addition, it will lessen the situations where you will find it necessary to reject others.

A Brief Reference To Your Liabilities (If Any)

If you have obvious liabilities, it is a good idea to state them from the very beginning. This will serve several purposes.

1. It will prevent a problem from occurring later on in the relationship because of this liability
2. It will instill a feeling of trust in the reader of the ad.
3. It will screen out people who are not interested in you.
4. The overt honesty will make your ad more interesting.

How to Refer to a Liability

Refer to it in positive terms. For example: You could say "a beauty queen I'm not," then follow up immediately with your positive qualities.

Emphasis On Your Positive Qualities

It is generally a good idea in classified advertising to call attention to your positive qualities.

This is particularly true if you have listed liabilities since it will tend to create a balance.

A Provocative Ending

It is generally favorable to have your ad end in a call for immediate action. It will result in your ad seeming stronger and more complete since it will have a beginning, a middle and an end. In addition, it could easily make the difference between a response and no response.

How To Make Your Ad Stand Out

The more visible your ad, the more responses you will receive. To make your ad stand out.

1. Have a border placed around your ad.
2. Use colorful words.
3. Place an ad that is longer than most ads.
4. Request that your ad be placed first, although this may or may not be possible.

ARE YOU THE RIGHT ONE FOR ME ?

Thirty-five year old professional Black man with some degree of depth and sensitivity seeking you Black woman age 25-35. An athlete I'm not but I'm dependable. You must be healthy and outgoing. No drugs. *Let's not miss out on a mutual opportunity. Write today!*

Why People Fail With Classified Ads

Each week a surprising number of people place classified ads only to find that either they get no responses, too few responses, or the quality of the responses to their ads are generally unacceptable.

The primary reasons people fail with classified ads are:

1. The ad was not well written. Either the message wasn't clear or the ad wasn't well organized.
2. The ad was not interesting enough to attract attention and may have blended in with the other ads.
3. The writer did not come through as attractive enough. Either there was too great an emphasis on liabilities and/or there wasn't enough emphasis on positive qualities.
4. The ad did not indicate clearly the writer's preferences. Generally the people who reply to your ad will be the kind of people that you specified, since most people will not answer an ad that requests someone completely different from who they are.
5. The writer aimed too high. What a person has to offer will, to a large extent, determine what he or she can demand and get.
6. The ad was placed in the wrong publication, therefore the

clientele of the newspaper and the writer of the ad were not
compatible.
7. The newspaper selected did not have adequate circulation.
Your possibilities are severely limited if there are not enough
people reading the newspaper.

An Additional Aspect Of Personal Classified Advertising

Many of the newspapers have installed recording equipment that
enables you to place a classified ad in your own voice. This is an
excellent idea only if your voice is an asset.

We will examine briefly how to improve your possibilities of
making this system of personal classified advertising work effectively.

*What are the factors that will determine whether or not you
succeed with a recorded personal classified ad*
They are:
1. The content of your message. This was examined at length.
2. Your voice and manner of speaking.

How Do You Improve Your Voice And Manner Of Speaking

First evaluate your voice. You can do this in two ways:
1. You can tape your voice and evaluate it yourself.
2. You can ask your friends and family how you sound.

What are the most obvious defects and how do you correct them
1. Too shrill
2. Lacking in color
3. Monotonous
4. Lacking in warmth
5. Enunciation unclear

Most people have relatively pleasing voices, but if you are not satisfied with your voice the functional exercise section outlines steps you can take. You can improve your voice. See the *Functional Exercises*.

PRACTICUM

SELF QUIZ

1. Why do you think that you can control a person's level of expectation with a classified ad?

2. How do you refer to a liability?

3. Why is it important to list your liabilities at the very beginning?

4. What is the best way to end a personal classified ad?

5. What are the most obvious voice defects?

FUNCTIONAL EXERCISES

1. List three important adjectives that describe your personality.

_____

2. Sum up your most important personal dislikes in one sentence.

_____

_____

_____

3. Describe your physical appearance in one sentence.

_____

_____

_____

4. Describe your personality in one sentence.

_____

_____

_____

5. Describe the kind of physical appearance you are seeking in one sentence.

_____

_____

_____

6. Describe the kind of personality you are seeking in one sentence.

_____

_____

_____

7. Compose an interesting headline.

_____

_____

FUNCTIONAL EXERCISES (If you record your ad)

1. Learn to listen to yourself.

2. Focus on enunciating clearly.

3. Practice reading poetry out loud.

4. Practice varying the pitch of your voice.

5. Practice using the lower tones of your voice since they are usually more attractive.

KEY QUESTIONS (To Ask Yourself Before Sending Out Your Personal Classified Ad)

1. Have I included all the components of a good ad?

2. Is the ad as brief as possible?

3. Does it portray me accurately, yet positively?

4. Does it make my preferences clear?

5. Does it make my dislikes clear?

6. Would I respond to this ad?

7. Would the kind of person I want to meet respond to this ad?

KEY QUESTIONS (To Ask Yourself Before Placing A Recorded Personal Ad)

1. Would I respond to my voice if I were a member of the opposite sex?

2. Do I sound friendly?

3. Do I sound like a warm person?

4. Do I sound interesting?

5. Do I sound like a person I could trust?

CHAPTER HIGHLIGHTS

1. You can greatly increase the number of people that you meet by using personal classified advertising.

2. An important advantage of using this method of seeking a mate is that you can design your ad to accentuate your positive characteristics and play down your negative characteristics.

3. An effective ad not only attracts attention, but indicates in detail who your are and what you want. It also indicates what you do not want.

4. There are special techniques involved in writing an ad that will succeed.

5. Your voice and manner of speaking will be of great importance if you decide to record your personal ad.

Chapter Seven

A LOOK AT INTRODUCTION SERVICES AND WHAT THEY CAN DO FOR YOU

BACKGROUND

This chapter will assist you in taking an in-depth look at introduction services so you can decide whether or not they are for you.

In addition, it will assist you in making effective use of these services should you decide to use them.

Your primary challenge is to weigh this option carefully and to be thoroughly objective about whether or not this is an approach for you. The difficult aspect of this challenge is to be sure that your final decision is not based on preconceived ideas.

You succeed with this chapter to the extent that you are open to learning and understanding the information about introduction services. It is important to weigh the advantages and disadvantages carefully before making a final decision. Should you decide to use this method of meeting a mate, it becomes an action chapter in that you are required to research introduction services thoroughly.

Introduction Services

I have always thought of introduction services as an option of the last resort until I began to research them. Although some of them are marginal and have received negative publicity, they have an impressive rate of success in bringing people together for marriage.

Although those of us who consider ourselves attractive may have some reservations about using introduction services, I felt an obligation to include them is this book because they are in reality a viable option for African-Americans. And like any other method of seeking a mate they have their advantages and disadvantages.

Let's take a general look at introduction services in terms of advantages and disadvantages.

General Advantages of Introductions Services

1. You can usually meet more people than you could by using your own resources. This is also true of the classified ad method.
2. You know in advance that persons you meet are available — or say they are.
3. Defenses and other barriers may often be minimized since both persons have openly admitted that they have a strong desire to meet someone.
4. Because of the expense involved you tend to attract serious clientele.

General Disadvantages of Introduction Services

1. The process may be time consuming.
2. Introduction services may be expensive.

Let's now examine the basic kinds of services, factors to consider before selecting a service, how to use them and why people fail with introduction services.

Basic Kinds of Introduction Services

The kinds of introduction services are many and varied. In addition

they serve a variety of populations. To simplify the maze, I will divide the services into two primary categories.
1. Those that work exclusively by mail.
2. Those that offer a personal interview.

Those That Work Exclusively By Mail

These may be computerized or non-computerized, they may service the general population or they may service select clientele such as the handicapped, the overweight, senior citizens, college students, high achievers, religious persons or creative persons.

How They Operate
1. You call or write for a questionnaire or application.
2. You return the completed questionnaire or application.
3. Your application is processed.
4. You are matched with potential mates.
5. You receive their names and telephone numbers.
6. They may in turn receive yours.

Advantages Of Services That Operate Entirely By Mail
1. You can meet many people quickly.
2. The cost is usually considerably lower (sometimes there is no cost to females).
3. There is some attempt to match in terms of basic similarities.

Disadvantages Of Services That Operate Entirely By Mail
1. There is little opportunity for pre-screening.
2. The matching process may not be intensive.

Introduction Services That Offer A Personal Interview

Introduction services that offer a personal interview generally do not use computers. Often they may have a psychologist or some other person to do the testing and interviewing of the clientele. Like the services that operate by mail they also may service specific populations.

How They Operate
1. You call or write for an interview.
2. You visit the office.
3. You may be interviewed, tested, photographed and/or video-taped.
4. You receive the names of persons with whom you are possibly compatible.
5. They in turn may receive your name.

Advantages
1. The selection process will in all probability be more intensive. Therefore, there is a greater possibility that you will meet someone with whom you are compatible.
2. In all probability more pre-screening will be done.
3. There may be more accountability.

Disadvantages
1. They may be quite costly.
2. More than likely you will receive fewer names.

Factors To Consider Before Deciding On Any Introduction Service

1. The criteria by which they match. Their underlying ideology should be known to you in advance.
2. The education and experience of the interviewer.
3. The type of clientele they service.
4. Their method of screening out undesirable persons. This is very important.
5. The methods by which they monitor their results.
   Let's go into these factors in greater detail.

Criteria By Which They Match

Each service has some criteria by which they match. It is very important to know the criteria on which they base their matches since this criteria may be sound or unsound.

Education And Experience Of The Interviewer

While no particular course of study prepares one for matchmaking, it is important that the matchmaker either have extensive experience and/or use the services of trained professionals. Training in the social sciences is most relevant. It is entirely appropriate when considering an introduction service to inquire about the training and experience of the interviewer.

Type Of Clientele They Service

Very few services can accommodate everyone. Usually the service is geared towards a particular clientele in terms of social class, education and personal appearance.

Be sure to ask questions about the kind of clientele they service. If the introduction service does not service people of your calibre it is highly unlikely that you will be satisfied with the people that you meet.

How To Know If An Introduction Service Accommodates Your Kind Of Clientele
1. The publication in which they advertise will often provide a valid clue.
2. The way advertising is worded is also important.
3. Office location can offer some clue to what you can anticipate.
4. Office decor — how the office is decorated is often indicative of the service you will receive.
5. The calibre of the staff will give some indication of the quality of services you can expect.

Method Of Screening Out Undesirable Persons

A question you may wish to raise to an introduction service concerns their method of screening out undesirable persons. That is, how thoroughly do they check the backgrounds of their clients? This is a very important question and the interviewer or proprietor should not hesitate to give you an answer.

Methods By Which They Monitor Results

If a given introduction service claims to have impressive results, and of course these are the only kind that you should contract with, find out how they monitor their results.

Is it by statistics? If so, who creates the statistics? Do they distribute evaluation forms? There must be some systematic manner of determining whether or not they are meeting their objectives.

How To Use Introduction Services

1. Be assertive about indicating what you want.
2. Give them adequate feedback. It is very important that they know how you feel about the people they introduce you to.
3. Give them adequate time. Enroll for at least a year so that you are not limited to the respondents of any given time period.
4. If you are using a service that operates by mail use only those with comprehensive questionnaires.

How To Maximize Assets And Minimize Liabilities With Introduction Services

Maximizing Assets

Specialization is the way to maximize assets when using introduction services. If you have specific assets such as wealth, beauty or high intelligence use a service that matches people who have these assets. These are the elite services that cater to a specific clientele.

Minimizing Liabilities

Ironically, using specialized services is also the key to minimizing liabilities. If you are an older person seeking a younger person try using services that make that sort of match. Your chances for success will be much greater since the terms of the match are understood in advance.

If you are overweight consider using introduction services that specialize in servicing overweight persons.

These strategies will maximize your assets and minimize your liabilities.

Why People Fail With Introduction Services

1. They did not give the service sufficient time. As a result they were limited to respondents who applied during a given period of time.
2. They did not fully investigate the services. Generally most services do a good job a few do not.
3. They use the wrong kind of introduction service. The kind of service that you use is very important. It is very important that you do some preliminary research before deciding upon a specific service.

PRACTICUM

SELF QUIZ

1. Why might you meet more people through introduction services than through more conventional methods?

2. What are the advantages of utilizing an introduction service that offers interviews?

3. Compare classified advertising with introduction services in terms of expanded possibilities for meeting a mate.

4. If you were an overweight person, how might you minimize this liability with an introduction service?

FUNCTIONAL EXERCISES

1. First write the names and addresses of at least four introduction services. *Note: If there are none in the yellow pages for your area, write to the nearest large city.*
   A. _____
   B. _____
   C. _____
   D. _____

2. Write for the brochure of all four introduction services.

3. Write a letter indicating what you are like and what you are looking for.

4. Practice what you will say to the people that you meet.

KEY QUESTIONS (to Ask Introduction Services)

1. What is the criteria by which they match persons?

2. What is the education and experience of the persons who make the matches?

3. What kind of clientele do they serve?

4. What is their method of screening?

5. What is the cost of their service?

6. How many matches do they offer?

CHAPTER HIGHLIGHTS

1. You can increase the number of potential mates that you will meet by enrolling in an introduction service.

2. Introduction services have many of the same advantages that classified advertising has.

3. Should you decide to try this method of meeting a mate, it is important to know what kind of service is the most appropriate for you.

4. An important factor in selecting an introduction service is their screening method.

Chapter Eight

TURNING ALMOST ANY PLACE INTO THE RIGHT PLACE TO MEET A POTENTIAL MATE

BACKGROUND

This chapter will assist you in making an accurate assessment of conventional places as they relate to you in your search for a mate. It will also assist you in examining the advantages and disadvantages of these places.

In addition, it will assist you in maximizing your assets and minimizing your liabilities.

Your primary challenge is to be totally honest in assessing your potential with respect to the conventional places which are available to you. In addition, your challenge is to select the places and situations where you are most likely to succeed.

This chapter calls for a great deal of thought on your part. Not only must you know and understand the information, but you must relate it to your individual situation before you act. Think about the premises presented here. Recall your past experiences and the past experience of others, try to think about the reasons for the underlying premises in a meaningful way.

Going to the Right Places

The kind of place where you search for a mate is very important. Not only will the place you seek a mate determine the level of your competition, it will also influence how your potential mate will react to you.

And yes, there is such a thing as being in the wrong place. Needless to say that if you are over forty and seeking a mate, the trendy discotheques are not for you. But there are also less obvious no-nos.

To use a place to your advantage you need to be aware of both your personal assets and liabilities. In addition, you must know in depth the kind of place it is. It is simple to maximize your assets and minimize your liabilities once you are equipped with the basic information.

Places And Your Decision Concerning Interracial Involvement

It is a matter of personal choice whether or not you will decide to become involved on an interracial level. This decision will naturally determine the racial mix of the places that you visit. The information presented here is basic and universal and will assist you in using places to your best advantage.

Let's now take a general look at situations and places where you are at an advantage.

Situations And Places Where You Are At An Advantage

Generally you are at an advantage in:
1. Situations and places where you have status.
2. Situations and place where there is some kind of common bond.
3. Situations and places where supply and demand work in your favor.

Situations And Places Where
You Are At A Disadvantage

You are at a disadvantage in:

1. Situations where supply and demand work against you. For example, if you are a female and you go to a place where there is one male for every 20 females.
2. Negative comparison type situations. For example, if you are not attractive and you visit a place where beauty queens congregate.

Let's now examine the advantages and disadvantages of specific places and situations.

The Church

The Church has historically been the foundation of our Community. Because of our pressing situations in today's world, the Church assumes a role of even greater importance. In addition to the obvious spiritual benefits, I can think of few places more suitable than the Church for meeting mates.

Advantages

1. The people that you meet will usually place a high value on you.
2. You can meet many people quickly.
3. The repeated contact offer opportunities for building bonds.

Disadvantages

Actually I can't think of any real disadvantages. However, as a person firmly rooted in the Church, I'll admit that I cannot be completely objective where the Church is concerned.

Being your most effective self

1. Involve yourself in the various activities and committees.
2. Be friendly.

3. Volunteer for central positions such as teacher or group leader.

Parties

Advantages
1. You can meet many people quickly.
2. You know immediately how the people you meet look.

Disadvantages
1. Personal appearance may assume too important a role.
2. The focus is on you exclusively. There is no mitigating activity. This may serve to create discomfort.
3. You have no way of knowing the people you meet in depth.

Being Your Most Effective Self
1. Keep the conversation light.
2. Avoid being too subdued. Because of the nature of a party, it's all right to overstate yourself.

Special Events (Sport Events, Theater Parties)

Advantages
1. The focus is not entirely on you. There is some activity or event. An immediate result of this fact is that you will feel more comfortable.
2. You can meet many people quickly.

Disadvantages
1. Since many special events are one time situations, you don't have the opportunity to become familiar with anyone.
2. Competition may be keen.
3. Personal appearance may assume a very important role.

4. Be aware of the fact that what is generally thought of as a liability may be considered an asset by some individuals. For example, a few young people might prefer an older mate. Also, some people do not consider excess weight to be a liability. Finally not everyone requires that their mate be physically attractive.

Maximizing Personal Assets

Before we begin to examine techniques for maximizing your personal assets, let's look at possible personal assets. They are:
1. Beauty
2. Wealth
3. Attractive personality
4. Intelligence

Of course there are many more but we will consider these four at this time.

To Maximize An Asset

1. You must be aware that you have it.
2. You must be aware of its value.
3. You must be aware of the fact that not everyone has this asset.
4. You must be aware of the fact that not everyone values this asset in the same way.
5. You should also know your trade off possibilities. For example, often beauty can be traded off for wealth.
6. In addition you must decide whether or not you wish to attract others because you have this asset.
7. You should also know the people most likely to value your assets — paradoxically, often those who have the same or similar assets appreciate a given asset as much as those who do not.

Let's now examine some specific techniques for maximizing your assets.

Beauty(should you decide to use this asset)
1. Go to places where the emphasis is on appearance.
2. Surround yourself with people who value this asset.
3. Refer to your appearance in your classified ad — if you decide to use this method of seeking a mate.

Wealth

(You may or may not wish to attract others because of this asset) But if you do:
1. Surround yourself with the symbols of wealth.
2. Associate with people who value this asset.

3. In addition, develop other assets such as an attractive personal appearance and/or a stimulating personality.

Attractive Personality
1. Visit places where the focus is more likely to be placed on personality.
2. Improve your personal appearance if it is necessary.
3. Associate with people who value this asset.

Superior Intelligence
1. Improve your personal appearance, if it is necessary.
2. Improve your personality, if it is necessary.
3. Associate with people who value this asset.
4. Visit places where the focus is most likely to be on intelligence.

There are many assets and liabilities and sometimes the line between what is an asset and what is a liability is not clear-cut. The information presented here assists you in making general judgments about how to use your traits and characteristics to your best advantage.

PRACTICUM

SELF QUIZ

1. What determines whether or not a place will be effective for you?

2. Why are you at an advantage in a situation where you have status?

3. What kind of people are you most likely to meet at psychology workshops?

4. Where would you go if you were elderly?

FUNCTIONAL EXERCISES

1. Send for information about as many conventional places for meeting mates as possible.

2. Again, list your assets.
   A. _____
   B. _____
   C. _____
   D. _____
   E. _____
   F. _____
   G. _____
   H. _____

3. List your liabilities.
   A. _____
   B. _____
   C. _____
   D. _____
   E. _____
   F. _____
   G. _____
   H. _____

4. Study both your assets and liabilities in relationship to the various conventional places.

5. Make a list of places where you are most likely to succeed based on the information presented.

A. _____
B. _____
C. _____
D. _____
E. _____
F. _____
G. _____
H. _____

KEY QUESTIONS (To ask yourself about a place)

1. Am I comfortable here? (Usually the wrong place is uncomfortable.)
2. Do I feel that my assets will be maximized here?
3. Do I feel that my liabilities will be minimized here?
4. Does this place reflect the racial mix of the people I wish to meet.
5. Are the people who come here likely to be interested in me?

CHAPTER HIGHLIGHTS

1. It is extremely important to select a place which shows you off to your best advantage.

2. If you are not physically attractive, it is very important to avoid places where appearance is emphasized.

3. Supply and demand will either work for or against you, at most places.

4. Most conventional places have built-in advantages and disadvantages.

5. It is very important to be aware of these advantages and disadvantages.

PART FOUR

SPECIFIC TECHNIQUES FOR MAKING YOUR RELATIONSHIP STICK ONCE YOU FIND A POTENTIAL MATE AND DEALING WITH REJECTION.

Chapter Nine

AFTER YOU MEET A POTENTIAL MATE

BACKGROUND

Generally this chapter will assist you in focusing on the factors that come into play once you meet a potential mate. More specifically, it will assist you in focusing on your strengths and weaknesses in terms of making a favorable first impression.

It will also assist you both in avoiding and managing rejection should it occur.

Your challenge is to be sufficiently objective so you can focus on any real liabilities that you may have in these areas.

In addition, your most difficult challenge is to understand that being rejected may not be related to how attractive you are.

This chapter is not an action chapter. It requires objectivity in terms of evaluating yourself and the kind of first impression that you make on other people. You succeed with this chapter to the extent that you are willing to be totally honest with yourself.

Managing First Impressions And Rejection

All relationships begin with first impressions. If the first impression is negative, usually the relationship will terminate at the very beginning.

In addition, no matter how attractive you are, if you meet enough new people over a long enough period of time you will more than likely experience rejection.

Therefore, there are two survival skills that you really need when you are searching for a mate, they are the skills of managing first impressions and rejection.

Let's examine both:

First Impressions

What Are The Factors That Determine The Quality Of Your First Impression

1. Your personal appearance which often will reflect your degree of Afrocentricity.
2. Your personality.
3. The immediate surroundings.
4. The frame of reference of the other person.

Let's now examine each factor individually.

What Is The Role Of Personal Appearance In Making A Favorable First Impression

Needless to say, it is most important to look your best. As we discussed before, the aspects that make up your personal appearance are:

1. Your clothing
2. Your hairstyle *(both of which will often reflect your degree of Afrocentricity)*
3. Your skin
4. Your build
5. Your facial features

6. Your accessories

We will not go into what to do about these factors but as is self-evident, you can control many aspects of your personal appearance by using professional services and studying the Black fashion magazines.

Personality

The second factor that determines the quality of your first impression is your personality. I have discovered that personality is expressed most clearly in your verbal and non-verbal communication and I will now examine both.

What Is Verbal Communication
Your verbal communication is:
1. What you say
2. How you say it (the sound of your voice and your manner of speaking).

If you wish to make a favorable first impression and pave the way for a real relationship, the most effective form of verbal communication, after the initial appropriate small talk and impersonal banter, consists of sharing your honest feelings about yourself and the other person. This will aid you in deciding whether or not you wish to continue the relationship. And if so, on what basis.

It is very important to take time to really listen and observe. To get the other person to talk, you can use open-ended questions. An open-ended question cannot be answered with a yes or no.

An example of an open ended question is: "What was your childhood like?" or "Why do you drive yourself so hard?" The answer to questions of this kind will provide valuable insight into the inner workings of the other person.

Non-Verbal Communication Consist Of
1. Your body language.
2. Your facial expressions *and*
3. Your general demeanor.

Your body language can vary from moment to moment and from situation to situation. These are your personal mannerisms and are to a large extent under your conscious control.

To make your body language work for you, be aware of it. Examine the message that your body conveys. Is it in line with what you want to communicate? If not alterations are in order.

Your facial expressions will usually indicate your mood and psychological state. To a large extent they are under your conscious control. Facial expressions can convey disdain, happiness, love or sadness.

To make your facial expressions serve your needs, be aware of them and be sure that they convey the message that you wish to convey.

Your general demeanor can be defined as how you carry yourself in general. Your demeanor will most likely reflect your self-image— how you see yourself. This will influence to a large extent how you will be perceived by others and how you will be treated.

I have examined personality factors. We will now go into how the immediate environment influences the quality of your first impression.

The Immediate Environment

The immediate environment plays an important role in determining the quality of your first impression since a pleasant environment will usually result in positive associations. Your immediate environment consists of your surroundings including both people and inanimate objects. How do you use your immediate environment to your advantage? Arrange it so that your meeting occurs in the most attractive surroundings possible.

Activities

Activities make relating easier and tend to make both people feel more comfortable.

Which activity should you select?

1. Of course the activity should maximize your assets and minimize your liabilities.
2. It should be in line with your natural assets.
3. The activity should also be in line with your innate skills.

4. The ideal activity in terms of making a first impression is the opportunity to communicate mitigated by an activity of some sort. The activity will ease the discomfort of conversational lags.

Frame Of Reference

Let's now examine how the frame of reference of the other person determines the quality of your first impression.

Each person that you meet comes with a history. He or she has had numerous life experiences that will influence how he or she perceives you. In addition to life experiences the people come with personal tastes, personal prejudices and a host of memories about other people.

Not only will you be compared with everyone he or she has ever known but you will also be measured up against his or her expectations.

How can you manage this situation and make a favorable impression despite the mind set of the other person?

To some extent you can preselect the people with whom you come in contact.

How To Pre-Select People

1. If you use the classified advertising method you can indicate the preferred background of the people that you wish to meet. You are most likely to make a good impression on a person with a background similar to yours.
2. You can re-examine the chapter on places and be very selective about the kind of places where you meet people. This will preselect to some extent the kind of people that you meet.

Despite the frame of reference of the person you can make a better first impression if you do not create elaborate expectations. You can do this by exposing your obvious flaws prior to the first meeting. This works best in the classified advertising approach.

Managing Rejection

No matter how much you succeed in managing first impressions, in all probability some rejection will still occur. Whether or not you manage it correctly will determine whether or not you will persist in your search for a mate.

General Attitudes That Will Help You To Manage Rejection

To manage rejection, see it as a natural part of your campaign. Then you will not be so disappointed when it occurs.

In addition you can manage rejection by depersonalizing it. The more you personalize rejection, the worse you will feel.

You can also manage rejection by realizing that people will often reject another person for reasons having absolutely nothing to do with the person. Sometimes a person is rejected because he or she is perceived as being too attractive. The rejector doesn't feel able to cope with the person's attractiveness.

Another technique for managing rejection is to avoid rejecting yourself. Because someone else may have rejected you is no reason to reject yourself. A way to perceive the situation is missed opportunity on the part of the rejector.

In addition you can control negative attitudes better if you put the reverse positive attitude in writing.

Also, if you think you have been rejected, you need to be sure that you have really been rejected. A person may not call you because he or she has lost your telephone number.

Finally, and this is optional, for your own personal growth, if you were really rejected you might want to find out *why* you were rejected. The feedback might be a valuable source of information and growth for you.

Situations Where You Are Most Likely To Be Rejected

1. When you are seeking qualities in others that you do not have. For example, if you are not personally attractive and are seeking someone who is.

2. When you are seeking persons with qualities that are not compatible with yours. For example, persons with vastly different background, they may not value your assets sufficiently.
3. When you are overly insecure. Your insecurities may cause you to act in ways that will ensure rejection. Generally, the most reliable buffer against rejection is high self-esteem.
4. When you are in the wrong place. (See chapter 8 on *"Turning Almost Any Place Into The Right Place To Meet A Potential Mate."*)

Who Is Most Likely To Reject You

1. Persons with low self-esteem.
2. Individuals who do not value your assets.
3. Those who have rejected someone similar to you in the past.
4. People who are overly rejecting.
5. Those with vastly different value systems from yourself.
6. A person vastly more attractive than you.

One important point on rejection.

Because of outside agitation and just bad press, African-Americans run the risk of rejecting each other — when it is not really what we intend to do.

To cut through this extraneous matter, we must communicate acceptance from the very start to someone we like.

Finally, rejection is never terminal. It is simply one person's opinion.

PRACTICUM

SELF QUIZ

1. In terms of making a good impression, what are the most effective forms of verbal communication?

2. What kind of activities work best on a first date?

3. What are three techniques for managing rejection?

4. In what kinds of situations are you most likely to be rejected?

FUNCTIONAL EXERCISES

1. Review the factors that determine the quality of your first impression.

2. List your strengths in terms of making a favorable first impression.
   A. _____
   B. _____
   C. _____
   D. _____
   E. _____
   F. _____

3. List your weaknesses.
   A. _____
   B. _____
   C. _____
   D. _____
   E. _____
   F. _____

4. Recall a time when you may have rejected someone that you really liked.

5. Think about the real reason why you rejected that person.

6. Can you think of at least two people who will value you for what you perceive as your weaknesses.
   A. _____
   B. _____

KEY QUESTIONS

1. What kind of first date will maximize your personal assets?

2. What kind of first date will minimize your personal liabilities?

3. Have you used every means possible to improve your appearance?

4. How can you utilize rejection to grow or move forward?

CHAPTER HIGHLIGHTS

1. The kind of first impression you make is determined by how you look, talk and act.

2. It is also determined by the activities and surroundings.

3. In addition, it is determined by who the other person is and what he or she is seeking.

4. It is important to learn to prevent and manage rejection if you are to succeed in finding a mate.

5. It is important that we not unintentionally reject each other.

PART FIVE

REVEALING DETAILS ABOUT SELECTING THE RIGHT MATE AND IMPROVING YOUR RELATIONSHIP WITH YOUR PRESENT MATE.

Chapter Ten

SELECTING THE RIGHT MATE AND IMPROVING YOUR RELATIONSHIP WITH YOUR PRESENT MATE

BACKGROUND

This chapter will offer you in-depth understanding of what makes a marriage or relationship last. In addition, it will assist you in clarifying your personal convictions about these basic elements. Finally it will assist you in terms of evaluating your compatibility with a potential mate and improving your relationship with your present mate.

Your challenge is to fully understand and accept your personal convictions as they are, not as they should be. In addition, you are challenged to make a match based on these convictions.

This chapter requires that you fully absorb and understand the information presented. In addition, relate this to your life experiences. It will take some time and work on your part to incorporate these basic premises into your belief system to the extent that you will act on them.

Racial Factors And Your Marriage

Racial factors not only influence whether or not you marry — they also influence the quality and duration of your marriage. Despite this fairly obvious fact, you as an individual can still determine to a large extent whether or not your marriage succeeds.

The Manageable Factors, Outside Of Race, Which Determine Whether Or Not Your Marriage Succeeds

The six most important manageable factors outside of race are:
1. Whether or not you are suitable for marriage.
2. Whether or not your marriage partner or potential marriage partner is suitable for marriage.
3. Whether or not basic compatibility exists.
4. Whether or not you are willing to work on your marriage constantly.
5. Whether or not there is mutual commitment.
6. Whether or not there is constant communication.

Let's examine each factor one by one.

Are You Suitable For Marriage

What are the most important evidences that you are suitable for marriage?
1. You have a realistic perception of what marriage is and what it is not.
2. You have an adequate amount of self-knowledge.
3. You are emotionally healthy with the appropriate amount of self-esteem.
4. You are willing to compromise.
5. You are a fairly effective communicator.
6. You really want your marriage to last.

Is Your Marriage Partner Or Potential Marriage Partner Suitable For Marriage

The most important evidence that he or she is suitable for marriage are:

1. He or she can fulfill your basic needs.
2. He or she basically likes you.
3. He or she basically likes the way you look.
4. He or she is emotionally healthy with an appropriate amount of self-esteem.
5. He or she has realistic expectations about marriage.
6. He or she has an adequate amount of self-knowledge.
7. He or she is willing to make compromises.
8. He or she is a fairly effective communicator.
9. He or she really wants the marriage to last.
10. You and he or she are basically compatible.

In Which Areas Should A Couple Be Compatible

The key areas where there should be some compatibility are:
1. The degree of Afrocentricity
2. Ideas about the relationship
3. Money concepts
4. Lifestyle philosophy
5. Children
6. Sex

Let's examine these areas in greater detail.

Degree Of Afrocentricity

As I have said, we differ greatly in terms of the way in which we view our Blackness and all of its implications. If a marriage or a relationship is to survive, there must be compatibility in this very important area. There will be an obvious clash if one partner is extremely Afrocentric and the other is not Afrocentric at all.

Ideas About The Relationship

A couple should not disagree on the nature of the relationship itself. In general they need to agree on the role each partner plays.

Relationships differ in terms of the amount of intimacy, amount of honesty, male or female dominance, amount of personal freedom of each partner, if and how anger is expressed, and in the amount of verbal communication.

Another area of concern may be whether or not a spouse can have friends of the opposite sex outside of the marriage.

Money Concepts

It is extremely important that a couple is in general agreement about money. Areas where differences may occur include who should earn it, how it should be used, who should manage it, how it should be managed, if and how it should be invested, whether or not any of it should be given away or whether or not it should be risked.

Lifestyle Philosophy

While a couple's views need not be identical in terms of what is an acceptable lifestyle, they should not clash. Areas where differences may occur include how recreational time is to be spent, whether or not there should be friends in common, what kinds of friends they will have, how the home should be used and the role of religion and/or politics in their lives. Ideally there should be some basic similarity in terms of how a couple views their life together. Glaring differences in basic perceptions about lifestyle can contribute to the failure of a marriage.

Children

A couple must first agree on whether or not they want children. Failure to come to some agreement about this basic issue can disrupt a marriage. If children are wanted there must be some decision made about how many and when. In addition, if children are wanted the couple must come to terms about what is acceptable and what is unacceptable in terms of rearing these children.

Sex

Since sex is more important to some individuals than to others a couple must agree on the relative importance of sex in their lives. In addition, since people vary in terms of both their interest in sex and their expertise, a couple must agree on what constitutes an acceptable or unacceptable sex life.

In addition, there should be some agreement in terms of what is acceptable and unacceptable behavior in terms of the sex act itself. Also to be considered are the frequency and duration of sex.

An Important Caution

The basic compatibility areas discussed are to be used as a guide. No two people are ever completely compatible. There will be differences and you will need to adjust and compromise. Even in highly successful marriages there is compromise and adjustment.

Tangible Methods Of Working On Your Marriage Or Relationship

The tangible work of a marriage or relationship, that is, what you must do on a tangible level to maintain your marriage, depends very much on who you are married to and what holds top priority in his or her value system. Marriage is a highly individualized institution.

For most segments of the population, the work of maintaining a marriage falls into the categories of:

1. Homemaking expertise
2. Sexual expertise
3. Professional advancement
4. Family development
5. Personal growth
6. Personal upkeep

Homemaking Expertise

To some people homemaking skills are extremely important and the important work of the marriage or relationship is providing quality meals and otherwise fostering a favorable home environment. To other people these skills assume less importance and may be delegated to competent professionals. Often homemaking skills tie in with family development. You work on a marriage or relationship where homemaking skills are a top priority by becoming more and more proficient at the skills involved in maintaining a home and family.

Sexual Expertise

Despite the popular belief that sex is very important, the importance that sex assumes in a relationship is highly individual. To some people sexual expertise is very important, to others it is not. In fact, sexual expertise may not even be desired in some situations. If sex holds foremost importance in your marriage or relationship your work is to become very proficient at it. There are numerous books and manuals on the subject.

Professional Advancement

For some people professional advancement is an important aspect of relating to their mate. To others it is not. In fact, to some people professional advancement and all that it costs may be viewed negatively. These people would prefer that their spouse place their priorities elsewhere.

Family Development

Family development which includes rearing the children and providing an excellent standard of living for family members, may be primarily what is expected of some mates. Consequently this is how they will spend their time. For other families this task may be delegated.

Personal Growth

Some individuals place a high priority on personal growth and development. Individuals who place their priorities in this area require that their mates constantly develop themselves intellectually and personally. Working on themselves and their minds is the important work of maintaining the marriage.

Personal Upkeep

Some people place their emphasis on personal appearance and are very much concerned about how their spouse looks. They may wish to project a certain image to the world. In marriages of this kind the individual's appearance and the appearance of the spouse is a major part of this image. The important work in a situation of this kind is grooming and other methods of personal upkeep.

These are the key tangible areas included in working on your marriage. Ideally one should excel in all. However, in reality, because of time and other limitations, few people can excel in everything. Therefore, it is most important to adjust your emphasis to your priorities and those of your spouse. Conflict occurs either when you fail to focus or you focus on the wrong area.

What is right and wrong? There are no clear-cut negatives or positives. What is preferred varies from situation to situation. Again, it is most important to know both your partner and yourself and what assumes top priority for both of you.

How do you find out what is most important to you? By doing the kind of self examination we have set in motion in this book.

How do you find what your partner wants? By constant observation and through asking questions.

We will now examine the less tangible ways of working on your marriage or relationship, but first let's look at an important component of long-term and successful marriages and relationships — **commitment**.

Commitment To The Marriage Or Relationship

Commitment is important in that it is the cement that keeps the marriage or relationship from dissolving when difficulties occur.

Commitment is simply a singular personal dedication to your marriage or relationship and your mate. This dedication results in your giving your relationship or marriage the top priority in our life.

More specifically it is a never faltering and intense desire to make your relationship successful. Ideally, this kind of commitment should be present in both partners. Whether or not his kind of commitment exists depends largely on your perception of relationships, the opposite sex and marriage, your level of psychological readiness and your prior conditioning.

Incidentally, commitment can be learned if you really want it. A very effective place to begin this learning process is in psychotherapy (couples therapy).

Less Tangible Methods Of Working On Your Marriage Or Relationship

Despite the extremely difficult circumstances of the African-American complicated by outside agitation and extremely bad press, you move forward in your relationships to the extent that you are emotionally healthy, psychologically aware and equipped with communication or people skills. Let's now deal with each requirement individually.

Emotional Health

You need a moderate amount of emotional health to function effectively in a relationship. It is emotional health that allows you to perceive yourself, your mate, and the relationship itself in an accurate way and to act and react appropriately. Without mental health your every effort will be undermined. Chapter 5 goes into tested methods of evaluating and improving emotional health.

Psychological Awareness

By psychological awareness, I simply refer to a basic savvy about what makes you and others tick. It is this kind of awareness that would lead you to fine tune your own eligibility, select someone with whom you are somewhat compatible and to bring a reasonable set of expectations to the relationship.

Communication

Communication skills are most important to a successful marriage or relationship. Both partners must know how to express their needs, likes and dislikes. They also need to know how to express anger appropriately, how to listen, how to stroke, and how to solve the problems that will occur in the relationship. There are effective and ineffective ways of communicating.

Danger

In every male or female relationship at some point anger will surface. Anger is a natural emotion that tends to mount when we are frustrated, tampered with or attacked in some way. Because of our experiences in this society, some African-Americans may store a residue of anger.

Anger can be redirected or displaced when the person who initially caused the anger is too powerful to attack. As is often the case with Black-Americans, this anger is then redirected at the people in our lives.

How do you deal with this anger? If anger is really intense and is experienced as rage, it is best to work it out in psychotherapy. If it is slight to moderate, the most important thing to do is to identify it and make some move to stop it at its source.

How do we do this in our relationships? The way to deal with this anger in our relationships is simply to make a direct statement about it to your partner. For example, you can simply say that you feel angry and specify the cause of the anger. That is all that is necessary. What you have done is communicated what you feel and why. If your mate is sincere about not creating anger for you he or she has all the information that is necessary. There is no need to scream threaten, or violate your mate in any way.

Expressing Needs, Likes And Dislikes

Everyone has needs, likes, and dislikes. In a relationship or marriage it is most important to know these needs, likes and dislikes. Not only is it important to make your wishes and preferences known, it is also important to know the wishes and preferences of your partner. How do you learn about the needs, likes and dislikes of your partner?

You can learn about you partner through observation but you don't know for sure whether the information is accurate. Therefore it is essential that both partners verbally express their needs, likes and dislikes. It is also most important to know how to communicate this information in a non-threatening way.

Listening
Listening is one of the most important of the communication skills and it is also one of the most difficult. Listening not only requires that you hear what your partner says, but also that you understand him or her. In addition you should make your partner aware that you understand him or her. You do this by paraphrasing what has been said, nodding and asking intelligent questions.

Stroking
Stroking, which is the simple act of giving approval to your partner, is vital to a good relationship. It is a basic need to know that you are respected and held in high esteem by the significant people in your life. Stroking makes people feel good and is a very important communication skill.

Many people are reluctant to give strokes because they may feel that stroking will be interpreted as a sign of weakness. But actually stroking is essential to a good relationship and will serve to prevent problems before they occur.

Problem Solving
Even in the best of marriages or relationships problems will come up from time to time. The ability to find effective solutions to these problems will often determine whether or not the marriage or relationship lasts.

Whether or not you are motivated to solve the problems that come up in your marriage or relationship will be directly influenced by your level of commitment.

Your communication skills play a very important role in your ability to solve problems. The most effective way to solve the problems that come up in a relationship is through honest communication about them. You need the ability to state the problem without placing blame or accusing your mate. You also need to recognize your role in bringing about the problem. You can then work toward an intelligent solution.

PRACTICUM

SELF QUIZ

1. What are the tangible methods of working on your marriage or relationship?

2. What are the less tangible methods of working on your marriage or relationship?

3. Why is it important for a couple to agree on a lifestyle?

4. What are the most important communication skills?

5. Why is commitment important?

FUNCTIONAL EXERCISES

1. Write a statement on your feelings about money and what kinds of attitudes are compatible with yours.

_____
_____
_____
_____
_____
_____
_____
_____

2. Write a statement on your feelings about Afrocentricity and what kinds of attitudes are compatible with yours.

_____

_____

_____

_____

_____

_____

_____

_____

3. Make a list of key elements that would contribute to a suitable lifestyle for you.

A. _____

B. _____

C. _____

D. _____

E. _____

F. _____

G. _____

H. _____

4. Make a list of key element that would contribute to an unsuitable lifestyle for you.

A. _____

B. _____

C. _____

D. _____

E. _____

F. _____

G. _____

H. _____

5. Make a list of sexual practices that you consider absolutely unacceptable.

A. _____

B. _____

C. _____

D. _____

E. _____

F. _____

G. _____

H. _____

6. Clarify for yourself your feelings about having children.

7. If children are wanted, clarify your feelings about rearing them.

KEY QUESTIONS

Money

1. Should money be saved, spent or invested?

2. If spent what should it be spent on?

3. Should any of it be given to charity?

4. Who should earn the money?

5. Who should manage it?

6. How should it be managed?

Lifestyle

1. How much time should we spend together?

2. How much time should we spend apart?

3. What kinds of friends should we have?

4. Should we have different friends or friends in common?

5. How should we use the time that we spend together?

6. What will the role of religion be in our lives?

7. What will be the role of politics in our lives?

Child Rearing

1. Should there be children?

2. If so, how many?

3. Who should be responsible for the tasks connected to them?

4. How should they be disciplined?

5. Who should be responsible for disciplining them?

Sex

1. How frequently should sex occur?

2. How long should the sex continue?

3. How much variety should there be?

4. What is considered unacceptable?

Relationship

1. Should a spouse have friends of the opposite sex outside of the marriage?

2. How honest should we be with each other?

3. How much authority should each partner have?

4. How intimate should we be with each other?

5. How much verbal communication should there be?

6. How much freedom should each partner have?

CHAPTER HIGHLIGHTS

1. There must be agreement on basic issues such as degree of Afrocentricity, money, lifestyle, child rearing and sex if a marriage is to last.

2. If there is no agreement, conflict will be the inevitable result.

3. Compromise is one way of compensating for lack of agreement.

4. While it may not be possible to marry someone totally in harmony with you, it is important to try not to marry someone with whom you will be incompatible.

Together we have explored enlightening points for making your most important decisions about mating and marriage, uncovered potent methods for mobilizing your total store of resources, examined workable methods and systems for finding an exactly right mate, gone into specific techniques for dealing with the situation once you meet a potential mate, and looked at revealing details about selecting the right mate and building more satisfying relationships. *WE ARE NOW ABOUT TO END.*

But before we do, I'd like to say a word to those individuals who have chosen to become involved exclusively with African-Americans. You have in a sense made a commitment beyond a simple commitment to your individual relationship. You have made a commitment to African-Americans as a people. If you have made that commitment it is important to verbalize it and celebrate it.

YES, we as a people can move forward in our relationships despite our current circumstances. You as an individual can meet the right person, develop an excellent relationship and marry if you wish.

As Hannibal put it —

"I WILL FIND A WAY — OR MAKE ONE!"

WITH THE HELP OF GOD!

OPTIONAL SELF-MANAGEMENT FORMS

OPTIONAL SELF-MANAGEMENT FORM

- Number One -

Select the method or combination of methods you plan to use for
seeking a mate.

1. _____

2. _____

3. _____

4. _____

Indicate rationale

_____

_____

_____

_____

_____

Indicate pitfalls

_____

_____

_____

_____

_____

Think of additional methods

_____

_____

_____

_____

_____

OPTIONAL SELF-MANAGEMENT FORM

- Number Two -

Deviations from schedule

_____
_____
_____
_____
_____

Amount of deviation

_____
_____
_____
_____
_____

Reason

_____
_____
_____
_____

Proposed methods for catching up

_____
_____
_____
_____

Ways to prevent recurrences

_____
_____
_____

OPTIONAL SELF-MANAGEMENT FORM

- Number Three -

Indicate problems you've encountered in seeking a mate.

_____

_____

_____

Describe possible causes

_____

_____

_____

Indicate action needed
1. _____
2. _____
3. _____

Indicate way in which action will correct problem

_____

_____

Indicate date action is to be taken

_____

_____

Indicate action taken

_____

_____

Indicate outcome of action

_____

_____

OPTIONAL SELF-MANAGEMENT FORM

- Number Four -

Description of unforeseen circumstances involved in mate seeking

_____

_____

_____

_____

Causes

_____

_____

_____

_____

Actions to be taken

_____

_____

_____

Date actions to be taken

_____

_____

_____

Plan to prevent recurrences

_____

_____

_____

OPTIONAL SELF-MANAGEMENT FORM

- Number Five -

Number of contacts planned

_____

_____

_____

_____

_____

Number of contacts actually made

_____

_____

_____

_____

Reason(s) for discrepancy

_____

_____

_____

_____

Corrective action

_____

_____

_____

_____

Plan to prevent recurrences

_____

_____

_____

_____

OPTIONAL SELF-MANAGEMENT FORM

- Number Six -

List weekly contacts

_____
_____
_____

List those completed

_____
_____
_____

Evaluate those completed

_____
_____
_____

List those not completed

_____
_____
_____

Reasons not completed

_____
_____
_____

Plan to prevent recurrences

_____
_____
_____

OPTIONAL SELF-MANAGEMENT FORM

- Number Seven -

Number of ads planned

_____
_____
_____
_____

Number of ads actually placed

_____
_____
_____
_____

Reason(s) for discrepancy

_____
_____
_____
_____

Corrective action

_____
_____
_____
_____

Plan to prevent recurrences

_____
_____
_____
_____

OPTIONAL SELF-MANAGEMENT FORM

- Number Eight -

Instances where I have put myself in situations where I am likely to be rejected.

_____

_____

_____

_____

Steps taken to prevent recurrences.

_____

_____

_____

_____

Have I reviewed situations and places where I am most likely to be rejected?

_____

_____

_____

_____

Have I reviewed maximizing assets — minimizing liabilities?

_____

_____

_____

_____

Additional methods of changing situation.

_____

_____

_____

OPTIONAL SELF-MANAGEMENT FORM

- Number Nine -

Number of people I have rejected this month.

With cause	*Without Cause*
1. _____	1. _____
2. _____	2. _____
3. _____	3. _____

Have I asked myself the key questions before each rejection? If not, why not?

Have these questions altered my views?

Think of additional methods to minimize the tendency to reject others.

Reward yourself for each additional method you thought of.

OPTIONAL SELF-MANAGEMENT FORM

- Number Ten-

Introduction Services

Service	Address	Tel. #	Follow-Up	Result
_____	_____			
_____	_____	_____	_____	_____
_____	_____			
_____	_____	_____	_____	_____
_____	_____			
_____	_____	_____	_____	_____
_____	_____			
_____	_____	_____	_____	_____
_____	_____			
_____	_____	_____	_____	_____
_____	_____			
_____	_____	_____	_____	_____
_____	_____			
_____	_____	_____	_____	_____

RECOMMENDED READINGS AND SELECTED BIBLIOGRAPHY

Adler, Mortimer, *How to Speak/How to Listen*, Macmillan (1983) New York.

Bach, Dr. George and Herb Goldstein, *Creative Aggression*, Avon Books (1979) New York.

Bach, Dr. George and Laura Torbet, *A Time for Caring*, Palacorte Press (1982) New York.

Bach, Dr. George and Ronald M. Deutsch, *Pairing*, Avon (1971) New York.

Bartlett, Steven J., Ph.D., *When You Don't Know Where to Turn: A Guide to Different Kinds of Psychotherapy*, Contemporary Books (1987) Chicago.

Bennett Jr., Lerone, *Before the Mayflower*, Penguin Books (1982) New York.

Bennett Jr. Lerone, *The Shaping of Black America,* Johnson Publishing Company (1975) Chicago.

Berne, Erich, *What Do You Say After You Say Hello*, Grove Press (1972) New York.

Berscheid, Ellen and Elaine Hatfield Walster, *Interpersonal Attraction*, Addison Wesley (1969) Reading, MA.

Branden, Nathaniel, *The Psychology of Love*, Tarcher (1980) Los Angeles.

Bolton, Robert, Ph.D., *People Skills*, Simon & Shuster (1979) New York.

Cialdini, Robert B., Ph.D, *Influence*, William Morrow & Company, Inc. (1984) New York.

Crouch, *"The Myth of the Black Male"*, Soul Illustrated (Spring, 1972) pg. 21-23.

Davis, George, *Black Love,* Doubleday (1977), Garden City, New York.

Desmond, Morris, *Intimate Behavior*, Random House (1972) New York.

Essence, *"Black Man/Black Woman - Closer Together or Further Apart"* (Editorial, October-November, 1973) pg. 38,39,72,73.

Fast, Julius, *Body Language*, M. Evans & Co. (1970) New York.

Gabor, Don, *How to Talk to People You Love,* Simon & Shuster (1989) New York.

Goldberg, Herb, *The New Male-Female Relationship*, William Morrow (1983) New York.

Grier, William H, MD., and Price M. Cobb, MD., *Black Rage*, Bantam Books (1974) New York.

Gurley Brown, Helen, *Having It All,* Simon & Schuster (1983) New York.

Hare, Nathan, *"For a Better Black Family"*, Ebony (February, 1976) pg. 62

Hare, Nathan, *"What Black Intellectuals Misunderstand about the Black Family"*, Black World (March, 1976) 4-14.

Harris, Thomas, *I'm O.K. — You're O.K.*, Harper & Row (1967) New York.

Jakubowski, Particia, Ph.D., and Arthur J. Lange, Ed.D., *The Assertive Option*, Research Press Co. (1978) Champaign, Illinois.

John, Ph.D., and Kris Amodeo, *Being Intimate*, Arkana (1984) London.

Kinder, Melvyn, Ph.D., and Conwell Cowan, Ph.D., *Husbands and Wives: Exploding Marital Myths* (1989).

Knapp, Mark and Gerald Mills, *Handbook of Interpersonal Communication*, Sage Publications (1985) Beverly Hills, CA.

Ladner, Joyce, *Tomorrow's Tomorrow: the Black Woman,* Doubleday (1971) Garden City, New York.

Lazarus, Arnold, *Marital Myths*, Impact (1985) San Louis Obispo, CA.

Livsey, Clara G., MD., *The Marriage Maintenance Manual*, Dial Press, (1977) New York.

Leo, John, "Therapy for Ethnics", *Time Magazine* (March 15, 1982), P.42.

Madow, Leo, MD., Anger — *How to Recognize It and Cope With It*, Charles Scribner (1972) New York.

Morton, Carol, *"Mistakes Black Men Make in Relating to Black Women"*, Ebony, (December, 1975), pg. 170-175.

Morton, Carol, *"Mistakes Black Women Make in Relating to Black Man"*, Ebony, (January, 1976) pg. 89-97.

McKay, Mathew, Ph.D., and Patrick Fanning, *Self Esteem*, St. Martin's Press (1987) New York.

Osborne, Cecil, *The Art of Understanding Your Mate,* Zondewan Publishing House (1975) Grand Rapids.

Parrish, Milton, *"Black Woman's Guide to the Black Man"*, Essence, (April, 1974) pg. 56-57.

Peale, Norman Vincent, "A Guide to Confident Living," Foundation for Christian Living, (1977) Pauling, New York.

Poussaint, Alvin, M.D. and Ann Poussaint, *"Black Women/ Black Men"* Ebony, (August, 1977) pp. 160-163.

Poussaint, Ann, *"Can Black Mariages Survive Modern Pressures?"*, Ebony (September, 1974) pg. 97-102.

Psychology Today, "Why Marriages Last", (June 1985) pp. 22-26.

Randolph, Laura B., *"Secrets About Black Man that Every Woman Should Know"*, Ebony (May, 1991) pg. 38-44.

Rogers, Carl, *Becoming Partners*, Delacorte (1973) New York.

Skolnick, Arlene, *The Intimate Environment - Exploring Marriage and the Family*, Little, Brown & Company (1973) Boston.

Smith, Wendell, "What Black Men Look For in Black Women", Red Sea Press (1989) Trenton.

Tournier, Paul, *To Understand Each Other*, John Knox Press (1967) Richmond.

Tyson, Richard and Joanne Tyson, "Sex and the Black Woman", Ebony (August, 1972) pg. 103-113.

Van Sertima, Ivan Prof., *They Came Before Columbus*, Random House (1975) New York.

Zunin, Leonard, MD., with Natalie Zunin, *Contact — The First Four Minutes*, Ballantine Press (1972), New York..

INDEX

Office, 75
Opportunities, 15, 40
Optimism, 25
Options, 71
Over weight, 76
Overly selective, 18, 33

P
Parties, 83
People, 52
Perfectionism, 44
Personal appearance, 15, 21,
23, 63, 67, 68
Personal characteristics, 39
Personality, 15, 16, 17, 43, 61,
86, 95, 96
Personality problems, 85
Personality traits, 55
Photographs, 41
Physical appearance, 63, 67,
68
Positives, 110
Positive qualities, 64
Practicum, 20, 28, 37, 45, 57,
67, 78, 90, 101, 114
Positive qualities, 64
Press, 43, 100
Problems, 55
Professions, 63
Proprietor, 75
Prospects, 52
Proximity, 35

Psychiatrist, 54
Psychoanalysis, 55
Psychological awareness, 111
Psychological readiness, 15,
16, 32, 33, 35
Psychologist, 54, 73
Psychotherapist, 54
Psychotherapy 21, 43, 51, 53,
54, 55, 56, 111

Q
Qualities, 46
Questionnaire, 73
Questions, 47

R
Race 15, 24, 28, 63
Racism, 22, 23, 24, 44, 48, 51
Realities, 32
Relationships, 50
Relative, 52
Religion, 117
Requirements, 24
Resources, 50, 51
Reward system, 53

S
Safe sex, 34
Savvy, 111
Science, 26
Screening, 75
Selective, 1, 15, 17

WHAT TOP LEVEL PEOPLE ARE SAYING ABOUT "BLACK RELATIONSHIPS MATING & MARRIAGE."

"ERNESTINE WALKER HAS WRITTEN FOR US A LOVE "TEXTBOOK"
"For the Black Single"
AWSOME and right on time a magnificent effort.

In this work Ms. Walker deals with the enigma of love and the human heart are also covered. The terrible turmoils involved in love and the pursuit of it.

Her work is to be commended for the forceful yet insightful and compassionate way in which it coaxes, cautions and coaches her reader into accepting the candid realities of life in todays' social setting, so necessary for the successful pursuit of a life mate.

UNIQUE but also enlightening, in that the work brings out only partially recognized or seldom recognized truths & facts of which one is that though it is an important human emotion, LOVE in and of itself, cannot solve all social ills and can fail, if not buttresses by other innate personal strengths.

PRACTICAL because it gives one the tools and materials for handling this very nettling subject. Whether it is himself or herself planning to launch a courtship or whether called upon to counsel or parent. As in that day when Dad or Mom calls in Johnny or Jane for that proverbial *Man to Man* or *Woman to Woman Talk.*

And Much, Much More...............

W. Moses Malloy
Former President, A.S.U.
New School for Social Research,
N.Y.U.

"The results are fantastic. This approach really works."

Kevin Williams
Bronx, New York
Student

Black Relationships, Mating & Marriage

ESSENTIAL INFORMATION PUBLICATIONS

50 Lexington Avenue • Suite 108
New York, New York 10010

YES, I would like to order additional copies of "Black
Relationships, Mating & Marriage"
My check or money order for $11.00 is enclosed

Name: _____

Company: _____

Address: _____

City: _____ Zip: _____

Phone: (___) _____

Special Wholesale Prices Available

MONEY BACK
GUARANTEE

If you are not
completely satisfied
with this book you
can return it within
thirty days for a
complete refund.